John Paul II, We Love You

John Paul II, We Love You

World Youth Day Reflections, 1984–2005

Edited by Barbara A. Murray
Saint Mary's Press™

Genuine recycled paper with 10% post-consumer
waste. Printed with soy-based ink. 5083200

The publishing team included Barbara A. Murray, development
editor; Laurie Delgatto, contributing development editor; Mary M.
Bambenek, development administrator; Lorraine Kilmartin, review-
er; Mary Koehler, permissions editor; Penelope Bonnar, copy editor;
Genevieve Nagel, photo researcher; Jonathan Thomas Goebel,
typesetter, designer, and cover designer; Andy Palmer, art director;
Alan S. Hanson, prepress specialist; manufacturing coordinated by
the production services department of Saint Mary's Press.

Printed in the United States of America

Printing: 9 8 7 6 5 4 3 2 1

Year: 20013 12 11 10 09 08 07 06 05

ISBN 0-88489-820-2

Library of Congress Cataloging-in-Publication Data

John Paul II, we love you : World Youth Day reflections, 1984–2005 /
edited by Barbara A. Murray.
    p. cm.
ISBN 0-88489-820-2 (pbk.)
    1. World Youth Day. 2. Youth—Religious life. 3. John Paul II,
Pope, 1920–4. Church work with youth—Catholic Church. I.
Murray, Barbara A. (Barbara Ann)
BX2347.8.Y7J57 2004
252'.55—dc22

                                                    2004014396

Dedication

For the young people of the Diocese of Lexington, Kentucky, especially those in the mountains, and for the diocesan Department of Education, 1993–2004.

I would like to thank those who took the time to contribute their experiences to this book: Kathleen A. Carver, Robert Collins, Chris Docherty, Andrei Gotia, Paul Henderson, Rev. Rafael Hernández Urigüen, Melissa Hines, Nicholas Huck, Colette A. Kennett, Gail Lubahn, Charles Mwongera, Anthony Ramuscak, and Gottfried Wölfl. The true impact of World Youth Day shines through their words and makes this book relevant to the lives of others. It is evident that their experiences and great love of Pope John Paul II inspired their writings.

I am grateful to Laurie Delgatto and Lorraine Kilmartin for their guidance and editorial knowledge, and to the team whose advice and expertise made working on this book so joyful.

I thank Sr. Judy Kramer, OSB, and Br. Paul Grass for their translation help and recommendations.

To the staff of *L'Osservatore Romano* for their help in securing important documents, especially to Marilia D'Addio for her timely responses and assistance, I offer a heartfelt *mille grazie!*

Table of Contents

Preface

The tears spilled down their faces; their voices grew hoarse from screaming their welcomes. They waved their bandanas over their heads, their action resembling the whirlybird that carried the only person who could draw the world's young people together in this celebration of their Catholic faith. Jumping up and down, they strained toward this man; they yearned to touch him, to see him closely, to be near him, even though they were far above him in the upper tiers of the stadium. Their excitement was palpable and contagious. With eager anticipation they watched the big-screen monitors that showed Pope John Paul II descending from the helicopter and walking to his pope mobile. As the Pope entered the stadium, those closest to his path reached out their hands, hoping to touch him. And when Pope John Paul II finally exited his pope mobile, mounted the stage, and greeted the thousands gathered, there was little doubt that the presence of God's love was flowing back and forth between the leader and his young Church. It was their moment.

This is my description of World Youth Day (WYD) in Denver in 1993, and yet, over the years, the same experience has touched thousands more in cities both familiar and unfamiliar to the world's youth: Rome, Buenos Aires, Santiago de Compostela, Czestochowa, Manila, Paris, Toronto, and Cologne. Each gathering has produced similar dynamics. This Pope loves the young people and they know it. And they love him and he knows it!

Pope John Paul II's accomplishments during his long tenure as pontiff are too numerous and too far-reaching to assess in this book. Certainly the creation of World Youth Day and its international gatherings marks his greatest achievement in his relationship with young Catholics around the world. Through these gatherings Pope John Paul II consistently challenges young people to follow Jesus and to live a life of commitment, hope, and love for all, especially for those the Scriptures call poor.

This book attempts to capture in words and pictures the magic, the mystery of the gift these World Youth Days have been for the young Church. *John Paul II, We Love You* is designed to sustain the good memories of those who participated and to remind all young people of the words of encouragement, trust, and challenge the Pope has directed to them alone. And finally, I hope this book inspires others to consent to and prepare for their own pilgrimage to future World Youth Days.

Though World Youth Day is commemorated annually, the international celebrations—those the Pope calls the young people to at a particular time and place—are usually held every two years. And the days are indeed celebrations. At every international World Youth Day gathering, the young people spend their mornings in catechetical sessions taught by bishops from all over the world. The afternoon and evening events they attend are opportunities for them to get to know one another and make friends, experience various cultures, and visit holy sites. At the heart of these days are the liturgical celebrations the young people share with their Pope. They experience the Way of the Cross, the Vigil, and the Sunday Eucharistic celebration with the Angelus. This is indeed a time when the world Church gather to proudly proclaim their faith.

These pages offer you a bit of the history of how the international celebrations came to be and perhaps a better understanding of the work of the Holy Spirit in that process.

To begin each year's World Youth Day pilgrimage, the Pope issues his "Message of the Holy Father John Paul II to the Youth of the World," presenting the theme for that year and spiritually preparing the young people to meet with him at the designated site. Each chapter in this book begins with excerpts from those messages. Following the Pope's words, young people who have attended various World Youth Days offer firsthand reflections, illustrating how those events have changed their lives and touched the hearts of many. My friend Gail writes:

> What a thrill to be so close to someone like the Pope and to be able to watch young people sing, chant, dance, and pray with such love and respect for this man. To watch a frail, yet strong man love and respect each of these young people was something I will never forget. He was one of them—maybe not in body, but definitely in faith and love for the Catholic Church. His spirit never faltered in each of the speeches he gave these pilgrims, and their respect for him never diminished.

Every attempt was made to solicit reflections from attendees of each international celebration of World Youth Day. I received responses from Kenya, Austria, Scotland, Germany, Canada, Spain, and the United States. The submissions appear as they were written. Few changes have been made to the grammar and no changes to the style, so that you can taste the remarkable international flavor so central to World Youth Days.

This book is a book of love—a book that shows how close Pope John Paul II holds the young people of the world to his heart. It is a book that shows the incredible love the young people return to him.

I hope your memories are enlivened, your commitment is deepened, and your challenges are accepted. May you be reminded in your reading that one day a young Pope John Paul II decided to call the world's young people together, and that call has made a tremendous difference in the life of the Church.

Barbara Murray

The Road to World Youth Day

Vatican II, WYD, and Young People

Did you know that the roots of World Youth Day can be traced to the Second Vatican Council? Many people are not aware of the document "Message of the II Vatican Council to Youth" of 7 December 1965. This brief document is clear in its focus on young people and its challenge to them to live a life in Christ:

> For four years the Church has been working to rejuvenate her image in order to respond the better to the design of her Founder, the great Living One, the Christ who is eternally young. At the term of this imposing self-examination of life, she now turns to you. It is for you, youth, especially for you that the Church now comes through her Council to enkindle your light, the light which illuminates the future, your future.

This document was released during a time of great change and upheaval in the world. The first and second world wars had concluded. The United States was recovering from the assassination of the young President John F. Kennedy and deepening its involvement in Vietnam. Social and cultural traditions and values were changing, and the Church looked to the next generation—the young people of that time—to be the beacons of hope in a world torn apart. The document tells the young people just what their Church expects of them:

> The Church is anxious that this society that you are going to build up should respect the dignity, the liberty, and the rights of individuals. These individuals are you. The Church is particularly anxious that this society should allow free expansion to her treasure ever ancient and ever new, namely faith, and

that your souls may be able to bask freely in its helpful light. She has confidence that . . . you will know how to affirm your faith in life and what gives meaning to it, that is to say, the certitude of the existence of a just and good God.

You can see that the Vatican Council II fathers had a lot of confidence in the young people of the time. They wanted the young people to know the basics of Catholic social teaching. They had faith that the young people understood and believed in respect for the dignity, liberty, and rights of individuals. In the face of those tumultuous times, the Council fathers believed that the young people had the strength to claim their belief in God's activity in their lives and in the world and that God was just and good. Their message to the youth goes on to express their trust and conviction in the ability of young people to stand firm in their faith in life and in what gives meaning to life:

> It is in the name of this God and of His Son, Jesus, that we exhort you to open your hearts to the dimensions of the world, to heed the appeal of your brothers, to place your youthful energies at their service. Fight against all egoism. Refuse to give free course to the instincts of violence and hatred which beget wars and all their train of miseries. Be generous, pure, respectful, and sincere, and build in enthusiasm a better world than your elders had.

And so the task of the young generation in 1965 was clear: to receive, announce, and work toward the reign of God. The young people were to be partners with God, their fellow Christians, and all people of faith in creating a more just, more loving, and more compassionate world— a world that would reflect the love of God for creation, the compassion of Christ for all people, and the will of the Holy Spirit in the hearts and minds of every disciple. You have a share in this same partnership. You too are meant to create a better world, and the Church looks to you with hope. Pope John Paul II has made the message of the Second Vatican Council his own and has shared it with the young people of all the World Youth Days.

The Impact of World Youth Day

Kathy writes:

My first knowledge of World Youth Day came when, as a member of the diocesan staff for youth ministry in the Archdiocese of Louisville, I learned that the Pope was coming to Denver in 1993. I remember the questions and uncertainty that raced through my mind. How many young people are going to attend ? What are their age ranges? How are we going to get to Denver? Where are we going to sleep? What's the vigil? Do we have the option of not going? (No.) So, I learned about World Youth Day by being thrown into it with 180 young pilgrims.

Those of us in the diocesan youth ministry community became knowledgeable about group travel in its many forms, altitude sickness versus homesickness, walkie-talkies and their limitations, the challenges of managing large groups of enthusiastic young people and tired adult chaperones. We also witnessed the power of young people when you gather in the name of Christ and the Church. We observed your openness to others of various cultural and social backgrounds—how enthusiastically you greeted one another and found something in common. And we were deeply touched by how you prayed together—often in different languages.

Without hesitation you shared your faith with one another, your love of Christ, and your deep affection for Pope John Paul II. Sometimes our best learning comes when we least expect it. Sometimes we learn in spite of ourselves.

One of the many graces of World Youth Day in Denver was that the Church in the United States, without reservation, fully embraced and supported its young members. One hundred eighty thousand young people from the United States gathered in Denver. Your presence in Denver was a testimony to the common, concerted, and committed effort of the adult faith community. Whether the need was financial, material, or human—the resources were made available. And when the Church's young members dispersed from Denver, you were welcomed home to communities that wanted to further the young faith alive in their sons and daughters. World Youth Day in Denver energized the Church community in the United States, focused on the good "in" and "of" the young, and validated the efforts of the youth ministry community. It served to integrate youth ministry much more deeply into the mainstream of the Church in the United States.

After Denver, the international celebrations of World Youth Day—and large group gatherings like the National Catholic Youth Conference (NCYC)—found their rightful place in a holistic vision of Catholic youth ministry in the United States. You may have been to NCYC and know what a unique experience the conference is. You know your faith has been grown and that you share the experience with other young people just like you.

In addition, the United States Catholic community became more and more aware of the full scope of these World Youth Day gatherings. We began to realize that young people from around the world were involved and that there was something to be learned by traveling to other countries. And we recognized the incredible dynamic of having the Pope and you, the Church's young people, together in one place. As a result, World Youth Days are now anticipated events in the life of the U.S. Church, and the messages from the Pope to the young people of the world are eagerly anticipated.

John Paul II wants the World Youth Days to become an opportunity for young people to encounter the risen Christ. He wants you to be able to meet and gaze upon the face of Jesus, the one who proclaimed in John 14:6, "I am the Life" and that "I came that they might have life" (*John* 10:10, NRSV).

Overarching Themes

by Kathy Carver

Are you aware that several themes consistently run through the various messages to youth that Pope John Paul II has issued to young people before every World Youth Day? Underscoring those themes is the constant and clear message that you—indeed all of humanity—are loved by God. There exists also the unambiguous call to discipleship, to follow Jesus on the journey of life. The Pope articulates his abiding trust and confidence in you to be fervent evangelizers of your peers, witnesses to the Gospel and to the redemption of Christ through the cross. He expresses his hope that you will play a central role in creating more just societies—of furthering God's reign. The principles of Catholic social teaching are deeply woven into all his messages to you. The Pope really wants them to be a part of your life.

The Pope is unshakable in his belief in you. He holds up to you only the highest of ideals; he demands of you no less than what you were created for. In speaking with young people, the Pope often speaks of truth, moral formation and ethics, the sacraments, vocations, freedom, and love. Let's consider his thoughts on these topics.

Truth

John Paul II consistently points young people toward Christ. He understands the questions that lie in your minds and hearts. The questions you ask are many and deep: you want to know who you are and what your purpose in life is, and you wonder who you are to become. You have questions about the world around you and your place in that world. The Pope loves your enthusiasm and recognizes your painful searching, and like a patient grandfather, he slowly steers you in the right direction. John Paul II knows that each of you must discern what God—this God who gave you the gift of life and who loves you beyond measure—is calling you to become. The Pope also knows that you are often bombarded with messages that distract, distort, or lead you away from the truth, the truth of your own being— whom you have been created to be—and the truth of Christ (see Pope John Paul II, XII WYD 1997).

Moral Formation and Ethics

Your adolescent and young adult years are very important years in your moral formation and education. John Paul II sets before you the goal of living a moral life—a life guided by clear principles so that you may form your conscience and become a person who lives with and models moral integrity. He helps you understand personal morality in your decision making, and he longs for you to comprehend how your own moral life affects the lives of others. The Pope sees being a person of moral principles as one of the most important contributions you can make to society and to the world (see Pope John Paul II, International Youth Year 1985).

The Sacraments

Pope John Paul II consistently invites young people to a deeper understanding of and fuller participation in the sacramental life of the Church. Through the sacraments everyone experiences the grace of God. This grace gives you courage and supports you in your life. It draws you more deeply to Christ, and it strengthens you for service to your brothers and sisters in Christ. In Baptism we all become new creations in Christ, people who are dedicated to responding to the call to Christian discipleship. Through the sacrament of Penance, we acknowledge our sinfulness before God and the community and experience the healing that is only possible through God. And in the Eucharist, our true source and summit of being, we all share in the death and Resurrection of our Lord and Savior Jesus Christ (see Pope John Paul II, XII WYD 1997).

Vocations

In Mark's Gospel (10:20–21) Jesus speaks to the young man and tells him to sell or give away all that he has and to "come follow me." Jesus's invitation was not just for that one young man, but for each one of you today. John Paul II reissues that same invitation to you—to follow Jesus, to be his disciple. Being a disciple of Jesus can take many forms. Your task is to quiet yourselves enough to be able to hear the call, to understand its meaning, and then to follow that call. For some of you, the call will lead to the ministerial priesthood. And some of you will dedicate yourselves to the religious or consecrated life.

Many of you will marry or remain single. However you experience the call, if you respond and follow it, you will live into your vocation and into becoming the person God has created you to be (see Pope John Paul II, VIII WYD 1993).

Freedom

Pope John Paul II often warns young people of the dangers that may deter you from your search for the truth. These dangers take many forms, from false beliefs and promises, to temptations, cynicism, and doubt. The Pope does not chastise you for your mistakes. Rather, he wants you to have a higher ideal, and he supports your right to exercise your own free will. He says free will is like an "immense gift," and he points you to the Holy Spirit who can guide you in choosing what is moral and what is good, over that which is sinful. By choosing the good, you will live more into what God hopes for your life (see Pope John Paul II, VI WYD 1991).

Love

True disciples of Christ are characterized by love, but not the love that is fleeting or fake. The Pope challenges young people to the love that Jesus lived out on this earth. That love is patient and enduring and is a love that seeks to meet the real needs of others. To discern others' needs—whether they are food or forgiveness, clothing or compassion, medicine or mercy—is to feed, clothe, and care for Christ. This is the true measure of Christian love and how you can partner with God in furthering the Kingdom (see Pope John Paul II, VIII WYD 1993).

The Challenge

To be communicators of faith, hope, and love to a world in such desperate need is no easy task. Christian discipleship, characterized by unconditional love and guided by moral principles, is rooted in the Paschal mystery—the life, death, and Resurrection of Jesus. Christian discipleship becomes real when it is guided by the Holy Spirit and lived through the grace of God. What greater challenge can be set before the youth of this generation in the ongoing aftermath of world events? The test for your generation is how well, how patiently, and how deeply you can love (see Pope John Paul II, IX and X WYD 1994 and 1995).

The Past Speaks to the Future

The Vatican Council II message issued forty years ago to youth is brief, yet no less eloquent in its focus and no less challenging in its vision than the more well-known documents of that council. These final words from Vatican Council II to the young people of the Church—echoed by Pope John Paul II throughout his World Youth Day messages and speeches—were, perhaps, the seeds of a new beginning:

> The Church looks to you with confidence and with love. Rich with a long past ever living in her, and marching on toward human perfection in time and the ultimate destinies of history and of life, the Church is the real youth of the world. She possesses what constitutes the strength and the charm of youth, that is to say, the ability to rejoice with what is beginning, to give oneself unreservedly, to renew oneself and to set out again for new conquests. Look

upon the Church and you will find in her the face of Christ, the genuine, humble, and wise Hero, the Prophet of truth and love, the Companion and Friend of youth. It is in the name of Christ that we salute you, that we exhort you and bless you.

Perhaps, in some mysterious and grace-filled way, the incarnation of World Youth Days began with the seeds planted in that address of the Second Vatican Council. The fruits of that document may have been etched into the heart of a young Karol Wojtyla, as he participated in the Council, to be celebrated in its fullness during his time as the leader of the world's Catholics.

One of a Gazillion Stories

. . . and Colette writes:

My first encounter with John Paul II turned out to be both the "high" and the "sigh" of nearly twenty-five years in diocesan youth ministry. The words *Denver* and *Cherry Creek Park* immediately generate a multitude of visual and emotional responses, even after ten years.

As I began the series of steps necessary to advertise our diocesan pilgrimage, arrange lodging and travel, and visit parishes to register youth and adults, I assumed that this journey would be like many other youth trips I had coordinated in the past. I soon discovered there was no outline, briefing, or workshop that could have adequately prepared me to utilize the multitude of both personal and professional skills that were mobilized as a result of Denver 1993.

For many grandparents and parents, the WYD pilgrimages with the Holy Father are an opportunity for their children and grandchildren to be part of history. I felt they were hoping that John Paul would prove faith is "caught not taught" and perhaps their own children would come home somehow transformed and strengthened in their Catholic beliefs. Family members were generous in providing financial support to encourage their loved ones to be part of this monumental gathering.

My own anticipation mounted as the International World Youth Day events approached. I dreamt for weeks of just getting one small glimpse of this charismatic man who was the epitome of what a youth minister should be. His ability to love our youth, and yet challenge them with great conviction to live out their Gospel Call, inspired me. What was it about this man that would incite youth to travel for thousands of miles, sleep in primitive settings, go without food and water, and shed tears at the mention of the name "John Paul II"? I wanted to know.

Our pilgrimage of over seven hundred teens and their adult chaperones from the Midwest was the trip of a lifetime. And I owe much of my spiritual journey on this Denver pilgrimage to a boy named William and a man named John Paul.

William was a stocky, young athlete who registered to "see the Pope" out of a sense of both curiosity and adventure. His parish fund-raising efforts were going well until life intervened. William was diagnosed with cancer. His body began to diminish from the ravages of chemotherapy and so did his spirit. His dream of "Denver" became elusive.

With collaborative efforts between William's parents, doctors, parish youth group, and the diocesan youth office, the dream was rekindled and William, with wheelchair and minus the hair on his head, boarded one of the deluxe motor coaches headed into the unknown of this international pilgrimage experience known as World Youth Day.

Fate smiled on William during the preparation for our trip as I was notified that [someone who had heard of] William's struggle with cancer, [arranged for] this young man . . . to receive Holy Communion from the Pope at the closing liturgy of the World Youth Day events at Cherry Creek Park. Upon hearing the news, William was speechless. Even with skin so pale that only traces of life could be captured, a blush seemed to appear each time William spoke of this remarkable opportunity as he anticipated the journey ahead.

In preparation, I deeply wanted to photograph this special moment in William's life but soon found obstacles in my path. Shortly after our buses settled in at the hotel, I began my quest. I went from phone call to phone call. I walked miles throughout the city to locate the World Youth Day office of the Secret Service; I waited in lines after filling out tons of paper requests for just one photo opportunity. And finally, I sat down at the table with the one agent who held the power to grant my request. I began to plead my case in simple terms, "Sir, I realize I'm nobody from nowhere USA, but it would mean so very much to me if you would allow me to take a picture of William receiving Holy Communion from the Pope."

He didn't say anything at first. I held my breath. What was minutes seemed to take forever as I tried to read his facial expression. I think the Secret Service must be trained to have one stoic look. After looking at my papers, he raised his head and spoke. It was confirmed! I left the table ready to explode with joy, and with a list of explicit instructions to prepare me for the big day.

On the morning of the closing liturgy with the Holy Father, I reported to the check-in point hours before others began to gather. The sun was so intense that day and I wondered how William would survive the heat. Then, the Secret Service agent came to get me. I was to be rotated into the media briefing in preparation of taking the picture. It was overwhelming to hear the multitude of rules and regulations provided to media representatives during the morning briefing. The list included the "dos and don'ts" of media coverage. One false move and we would be removed from the rotation.

I have been an avid photographer since childhood but in comparison, my tiny SLR camera seemed powerless against the mega-lenses of the national press photographers who surrounded me. I felt certain they were wondering what I was doing among them.

The moment had arrived. We moved quickly to the staging area and positioned ourselves against the wall, as instructed. Shouts of "I see him!" began to fill my ears. But all had not gone as planned. John Paul II chose to leave the safety of the pope mobile and walk to the staging area. There was a frenzy of Secret Service commotion as I heard the radios squeal, "He's walking . . . he's walking." Before I could comprehend what was happening, there he was. The cheers around me were surreal. I felt such solitude as I observed the Holy Father move toward the stage. Life happened in slow motion and it appeared that time stood still. I was humbled and in awe as he passed directly in front of me!

Because of the length of the closing liturgy, I was moved out of the media area back to the holding area to await yet another media rotation. I prayed that they would not forget about me. I strained to see what was happening. Was it time? Had I missed the opportunity?

Another Secret Service agent pointed at me and said, "You; you're in the next rotation." I can't describe what I felt when I saw William. There he was. He began his climb up the steps to the Holy Father. (Believe it or not, the Holy Father had asked if he should come down the steps to William or if William wanted to climb. And William's athletic spirit chose climbing.)

William's leg was dragging due to the brace that supported his movement. His face was bright red, reflecting time spent in the blazing sun. As he passed near me, I wanted to call his name but that would have broken protocol and cost me my chance to experience this moment. I couldn't make that sacrifice.

William's steps were slow and deliberate. I held my breath as he picked up each foot and moved forward. Suddenly, he hesitated and reached for a step; William was falling. I gasped as I watched the volunteer escort support him to his feet. My heart was pounding. I murmured to myself, "William, you can do this." And I thought: JESUS FALLS THE FIRST TIME. What took minutes seemed like hours. My heart was pounding as William cautiously conquered each step. The Holy Father stood at the top looking down with a face that expressed both encouragement and compassion. The music of the choir swelled. My camera was shaking from my trembling hands. I could barely keep my finger on the shutter. Tears clouded my view.

I couldn't see William's face directly. But as he received the Eucharist and turned from the Holy Father to begin his descent, his face was glowing with life. If there is a "look" that depicts living a dream, I saw that look in William.

I fell to my knees and put my head onto my lap and offered a prayer of thanksgiving.

And this is my story. On a hot summer day in 1993, the lived reality of the Paschal mystery embraced my very soul. I witnessed the journey from a diagnosis of cancer to a moment of divine grace. William had suffered greatly and had given up much in the journey to get to Denver. But his spirit truly soared on that special day in Cherry Creek.

I have relived those moments frequently throughout the past ten years. Cherry Creek will always be part of my spiritual journey. And as for William, well, William has married. In fact, he is a new father. A miracle baby in many ways. Although I rarely encounter William these days, our hearts shall forever be joined by our International World Youth Day experience. For hope was born anew in Cherry Creek through a man named John Paul II and the power of that Paschal mystery.

The Seeds of World Youth Day

(1984—1985)

Saint Peter's Square, Rome, Italy
(Palm Sunday, 15 April 1984)

The Movement of the Holy Spirit: 1984 and 1985

The Presentation of the Cross

During the 1983–1984 Holy Year of Redemption, Pope John Paul II requested that a cross be placed near the main altar of Saint Peter's Basilica. When that Holy Year celebration concluded, the Holy Father gave the cross, which stood 3.8 meters, or almost 12½ feet, tall, to the youth of San Lorenzo Youth Centre in Rome. On 22 April 1984, the Holy Father said these words to those gathered at the basilica:

> My dear young people, at the conclusion of the Holy Year, I entrust to you the sign of this Jubilee Year: the Cross of Christ! Carry it throughout the world as a symbol of Christ's love for humanity, and announce to everyone that only in the death and resurrection of Christ can we find salvation and redemption.

That was it. The first step. The moment when the seed of World Youth Day began to germinate. From that directive of the Pope to the young people of San Lorenzo, who knew we would come to celebrate the twentieth anniversary of that cross? Who knew?

Saint Peter's Square, Rome, Italy
(Palm Sunday, 31 March 1985)

An International Youth Gathering

In the Beginning

From his participation in the Second Vatican Council to the present, Pope John Paul II has been a consistent and staunch advocate for young people. At his behest, young people met with him in 1985, the year the United Nations proclaimed International Youth Year. For him, World Youth Days are the moments when young people of various cultural, political, and social backgrounds can interact with and learn from one another. John Paul II clearly desires that these annual exchanges are vehicles through which the young people experience personal growth:

> In a special way, however, we study the human person through contact with others. Being young should enable you to "increase in wisdom" through this contact. For youth is the time for new contacts, new companionships and friendships, in a circle wider than the family alone. . . . This whole youthful experience will be useful to the extent that it gives you the ability to make critical judgments and above all the capacity of discernment in all things human." (*Dilecti Amici,* 31 March 1985)

Pope John Paul II twice invited young people to Rome. On 22 May 1983, he invited them "for a prayer meeting, for sharing, conversion, and joy." On 25 November 1984, the Holy Father invited young people to come to Rome on Palm Sunday to "celebrate, proclaim, bear witness together 'that Christ is our peace.'"

The actual proclamation for World Youth Day occurred on 20 December 1985 when the Pope addressed the College of Cardinals and the Roman Curia. But the Pope credits young people themselves with the creation of World Youth Days:

> At the very beginning, during the Jubilee Year of the Redemption, and then again for the International Year of Youth, sponsored by the United Nations (1985), young people were invited to Rome. This was the beginning. *No one invented the World Youth Days. It was the young people themselves who created them.* Those Days, those encounters, then became something desired by young people throughout the world.
>
> The World Youth Days have become a great and fascinating witness that young people give of themselves. They have become a powerful means of evangelization. *In the young there is, in fact, an immense potential for good and for creative possibility.* Whenever I meet them in my travels throughout the world, I *wait first of all to hear what they want to tell me about themselves,* about their society, about their Church. And I always point out: "What I am going to say to you is not as important as what you are going to say to me. You will not necessarily say it to me in words; you will say it to me by your presence, by your song, perhaps by your dancing, by your skits, and finally by your enthusiasm." (*Crossing the Threshold of Hope,* pages 124–125)

Since the very beginning of John Paul II's pontificate, young people have been an important gift to the Church. Over two hundred homilies, speeches, and messages have been created and delivered by the Pope to communicate directly with the youth.

Pope John Paul II Proclaims World Youth Day

On 31 March 1985, Pope John Paul II issued *Dilecti Amici*, his apostolic letter to the youth of the world on the occasion of the International Youth Year. In the letter, the Pope addressed young people in a significant manner, challenging them with his words.

And so the Pope says:

> The first and principal wish that the Church expresses for you young people, through my lips, in this Year dedicated to Youth, is this: that you should "always be prepared to make a defence to any one who calls you to account for the hope that is in you" (*1 Peter* 3:15).
>
> This is the exhortation that I address to you young people at the beginning of the present year. 1985 has been proclaimed by the United Nations Organization International Youth Year, and this is of great significance, first of all for yourselves, and also for people of all ages—individuals, communities and the whole of society. It is of particular significance also for the Church, as the custodian of fundamental truths and values and at the same time as the minister of the eternal destinies that man the great human family have in God himself. . . .
>
> It is easy to understand why the Church attributes special importance to the period of youth as a key stage in the life of every human being. You young people are the ones who embody this youth: you are the youth of the nations and societies, the youth of every family and of all humanity; you are also the youth of the Church. We are all looking to you, for all of us, thanks to you, in a certain sense continually become young again. So your youth is not just your own property, your personal property

or the property of a generation: it belongs to the whole of that space that every man traverses in his life's journey, and at the same time it is a special possession belonging to everyone. It is a possession of humanity itself. . . .

The question about the value of life, about the meaning of life, forms part of the singular treasure of youth. It comes from the very heart of the riches and the anxieties linked with that plan for life that must be undertaken and carried out. Still more so, when youth is tested by personal suffering, or is profoundly aware of the suffering of others; when it experiences a powerful shock at the sight of the many kinds of evil that exist in the world; finally, when it comes face to face with the mystery of sin, of human iniquity. Christ's reply is this: "Only God is good"; only God is love. This reply may seem difficult, but at the same time it is firm and it is true; it bears within itself the definitive solution. How I pray that you, my young friends, will hear Christ's reply in the most personal way possible. . . .

It is my hope that your youth will provide you with a sturdy basis of sound principles, that your conscience will attain in these years of your youth that mature clearsightedness that during your whole lives will enable each one of you to remain always a "person of conscience", a "person of principles", a "person who inspires trust", in other words, a person who is credible. The moral personality formed in this way constitutes the most important contribution that you can make to life in the community, to the family, to society, to professional activity and also to cultural and political activity, and finally to the community of the Church—to all those spheres with which you are already or will one day be connected. . . .

Young people, one might say, have an inborn "sense of truth". And truth must be used for freedom; young people also have a spontaneous "desire for freedom". And what does it mean to be free? It means to know how to use one's freedom in truth—to be "truly" free. To be truly free does not at all mean doing everything that pleases me, or doing what I want to do. Freedom contains in itself the criterion of truth, the discipline of truth. To be truly free means to use one's own freedom for what is a true good. Continuing therefore: to be truly free means to be a person of upright conscience, to be responsible, to be a person "for others". . . .

Pray and learn to pray! Open your hearts and your consciences to the one who knows you better than you know yourselves. Talk to him! Deepen your knowledge of the word of the living God by reading and meditating on the Scriptures. . . .

All of you live every day among those dear to you. But this circle gradually expands. An ever increasing number of people come to share in your life, and you yourselves discern the outlines of a communion that unites you with them. This is almost always a community that in some way is made up of different elements. It is differentiated in the way that the Second Vatican Council perceived and declared in its Dogmatic Constitution on the Church and in the Pastoral Constitution on the Church in the Modern World. In some cases your young years are being lived in environments that are uniform from the point of view of religious confession, in others where there are differences of religion, or even on the border-line between faith and unbelief, the latter being in the form either of agnosticism or of atheism in its various expressions.

It seems nevertheless that when faced by certain questions these many different communities of young people feel, think and react in a very similar way. For example, it seems that they are all united by a common attitude towards the fact that hundreds of thousands of people are living in extreme poverty and are even dying of hunger, while at the same time vast sums are being spent on the production of nuclear weapons, the stocks of which at this very moment are capable of bringing about humanity's self-destruction. There are other similar tensions and threats, on a scale never before known in the history of humanity. This is dealt with in the already mentioned Message for the New Year, so I will not go into the problems again here. We are all aware that the horizon of the lives of the billions of people who make up the human family at the close of the second millennium after Christ seems to portend the possibility of calamities and catastrophes on a truly apocalyptic scale.

In this situation you young people can rightly ask the preceding generations: How have we come to this point? Why have we reached such a degree of peril for humanity all over the world? What are the causes of the injustice that affronts our eyes? Why are so many dying of hunger? Why so many millions of refugees at the different borders? Why so many cases in which fundamental human rights are trampled on? So many prisons and concentration camps, so much systematic violence and the murder of innocent people, so much abuse of men and women, so much torture and torment inflicted on human bodies and human consciences? And in the midst of all this there is also the fact of young men who have on their consciences so many innocent victims, because it has been instilled into them that only in this way—through organized terrorism—can the world be made a better place. So again you ask: Why?

You young people can ask all these questions, indeed you must! For this is the world you are living in today, and in which you will have to live tomorrow, when the older generation has passed on. So you rightly ask: Why does humanity's great progress in science and technology—which cannot be compared with any preceding period of history—why does man's progress in mastering the material world turn against humanity itself in so many ways? So you rightly ask, though also with a sense of inner foreboding: Is this state of affairs irreversible? Can it be changed? Shall we succeed in changing it?

You rightly ask this. Yes, this is the fundamental question facing your generation. . . .

Precisely on this day the Bishop of Rome prays together with you for all the young people of the world, for each and every one. We are praying in the community of the Church so that—against the background of the difficult times in which we live—you "may always be prepared to make a defence to anyone who calls you to account for the hope that is in you" (1 Peter 3:15). Yes, precisely you, because on you depends the future, on you depends also the end of this millennium and the beginning of the next. . . .

I repeat these words of the Mother of God and I address them to you, to each one of you young people: "Do whatever Christ tells you." And I bless you in the name of the Most Holy Trinity. Amen.

And the Young People Reflect

Charles writes:

According to my reflection, 1985 was a very important year for the young people, especially here in sub-Saharan Africa [Kenya]. This is because two unique figures joined hands to give us hope and encouragement in our lives. I am speaking of our beloved Pope and the United Nations Organisation. The Church works closely with the UN. These people have brought hope into our lives. They give us food when the famine sweeps; they treat us in their clinics when we are attacked by soldiers and other criminals. They give us clothes to cover our bodies. They give us shelter in the refugee camps, when our homes are burnt down. The Catholic Church, being headed by the Pope, has tried to come to the aid of young people affected by these calamities. We have more refugee camps than good family homes! Talking of tribal animosity, which I have been a victim of—many areas we have ruins of what used to be huts and we have skeletons of both people and animals. The Church has opened many rehabilitation centers to bring the young people affected to their normal way of life. What can finish our bitter memories other than kind words, tender care and concern of Catholic Nuns, Brothers and Priests working here? When we see them in my place, we say that "they have brought us what the Pope gave them". It is true because it's due to the well-organised channels by our Pope that many ends of the World can get the Good News as Jesus commanded his Apostles to do (see *Matthew* 28:19).

. . . and Gottfried writes:

When I look now back, I see clearly how God was leading me through my life. Always when I thought there is no way, or I meant that God is not answering my prayers, God was already right by my side leading me the way! Thank you, Lord, for all you have done in my life!

. . . and Melissa writes:

The Holy Father challenged us to find Christ in the Eucharist and each other. He passionately advocated the truth of our vocation—to be God's people and to shine like we are sons and daughters of a King, because, literally, we are! John Paul II reminded us that with the Holy Spirit within us, we could motivate those around us and the countries we inhabit to love better and live better. Our Holy Father wanted us to build a civilization of love and to help our world see the deep need for Jesus.

The youth ministry at my church cultivated the seeds my parents and grandparents had planted within me. The program gave me an outlet for healthy socializing with my peers, opportunities to serve the community and parish while developing my own talents and most importantly, helped encourage a method to express my own relationship with Jesus Christ. In many creative ways, my adult leaders had devised a system, which taught youth how to open their eyes and see the work of God in life's events. They also taught us how to develop the gifts of communication and outreach to others our age, at the same time, building meaningful relationships with us as good mentors. High school pressures were a little easier to bear because they had built an environment and community which promoted love and respect to all who came through their doors.

. . . and Andrei writes:

The Pope, as a true shepherd, knows very well the world his flock lives in: probably never before was the family more under threat than it is today. Media and the society entice young people today daily in various ways to use each other, especially sexually, to seek pleasure at all costs, to see in children a burden to be dealt away with, not a blessing to be sought, to avoid effort, to be unfaithful to each other. Being a follower of Christ in today's society is an act of heroism.

. . . and Father Hernández writes:

It seems to me that almost all of us are in agreement that thanks to the impulse of John Paul II, Christian educators have begun to see youth not so much as a problem but as a generation which bears rich values and from them one can learn a great deal. John Paul II being priest, teacher, and bishop has maintained a listening stance of dialogue and of affection and respect with the youth. This has been his position all during his pontificate.

In his homilies and talks, John Paul II has maintained a personalized and human dimension of the Christian faith and above all he offers a model of his own authentic life, demanding yet understanding the youth. He speaks heart to heart with each of the young people here. To pray, meditate on the gospel, and live nourished by the Eucharist in an adoring attitude, considering it a fountain of most generous dedication to others has been the way in which John Paul II showed the youth how to rediscover their own faith.

Buenos Aires, Argentina
(11–12 April 1987)

Theme: "We ourselves have known and put our faith in God's love towards ourselves" (*1 John* 4:16).

And so the Pope says:

Dear young people, my friends,

On the 8th of June this year I had the immense joy of announcing that the next World Day of Youth will be celebrated at Buenos Aires on Palm Sunday 1987. This will be the moment in which, with the help of God, I shall culminate my apostolic visit to the countries of the cone of South America: Uruguay, Chile and Argentina.

At Buenos Aires I shall have the great joy of meeting not only the young people of Argentina, but also many other young people coming from the whole of the Latin-American continent and other countries in the world. In this much awaited meeting, we shall all feel in communion of prayer, friendship and brotherhood, responsibility and commitment, with the other young people who, gathered round their pastors, shall celebrate this Day in local Churches throughout the world. We shall also feel in union with all those who are seeking God with a sincere heart and who wish to dedicate their youthful energies to the construction of a more just and fraternal society.

It is significant that the World Day of Youth should this time have the centre of its celebration in Latin America, the majority of whose population consists of young people, who are the animators and future protagonists of what has been called the "continent of hope". The Church of Latin America, which proclaimed its "preferential option for the young" at Puebla (Mexico), is preparing itself for a "new evangelization" to rediscover its roots and rejuvenate the Christian tradition and culture of its people on the threshold of the "half millennium" of its first evangelization. [The bishops' conference at Puebla, Mexico, gave birth to the term "preferential option for the poor." The same conference also produced the lesser-known phrase "preferential option for the young."—Ed.]

Our words are intended as an appeal to young people everywhere, from the North and the South, from the East and the West, to join together, for it is they who will be the men and women of the year 2000 and whom the Church recognizes and welcomes with hope.

I would like to remind you of a thought I expressed in my first Encyclical "Man cannot live without love" (*Redemptor Hominis*, number 10).

It is in this period of our life [the life of the young] that we most have a need to feel ourselves recognized, supported, listened to and loved. You know very well, in the depths of your heart, that the satisfactions afforded by a superficial hedonism are ephemeral and leave nothing but emptiness in our soul; that it is illusory to enclose ourselves in the shell of our own egoism; that all indifference and scepticism contradict the noble aspirations of a love that knows no frontiers; and that the temptations of violence and ideologies which deny God can only lead to a dead end.

I want to appeal to you to grow in humanity, to give absolute priority to the values of the spirit, and to transform yourselves . . . by increasingly recognizing and accepting the presence of God in your life: the presence of a God who is Love, of a Father who loves each one of us for the whole of eternity, who created us by love and who loved us so much that he gave up his Only Son to forgive us our sins, to reconcile us to him, and to enable us to live with him in a communion of love which will never end. The World Day of Youth should therefore prepare us all to accept this gift of the love of God by which we are transformed and by which we are saved. The world anxiously awaits our witness of love, a witness born from a deep personal conviction and a sincere act of love and faith in the Risen Christ. This is what is meant by experiencing love and believing in it.

Our celebrations will also have a clearly community dimension. This is an inescapable need of the love of God and the communion of those who feel themselves to be [children] of the same Father, brothers [and sisters] in Jesus Christ and united by the power of the Spirit. By forming part of the great family of the redeemed and by being living members of the Church, you will experience, during this World Day, the enthusiasm and joy of the love of God by which you are called to unity and solidarity.

This is a call that excludes no one. On the contrary, it is one that transcends frontiers and is addressed to all young people without distinction. It is a call that strengthens and renews the bonds by which young people are united. In these conditions, it is essential that the bonds that unite them be particularly strong and operative with the young who are suffering from unemployment, who are living in poverty or solitude, who feel themselves marginalized or who bear the heavy cross of sickness.

It is essential, too, that this message of friendship also reach those who do not accept religious faith. Charity does not compromise with error, but it goes out towards everyone to open up the paths of conversion. How splendid and luminous are the words addressed to us in this respect by Saint Paul in his hymn to charity! (cf. *1 Corinthians* 13) May they be for you a programme of conduct and resolute commitment for your present and future life!

The love of God poured into our hearts by the Holy Spirit (cf. *Romans* 5:5) must deepen our awareness of the blatant threats posed by hunger and war, the scandalous disparities between opulent minorities and poor peoples, the violations of human rights and fundamental human liberties, including man's right to religious freedom, and actual or potential manipulations of his dignity.

May Jesus be the "cornerstone" (cf. *Ephesians* 2:20) of your life and of the new civilization you are called to build in a spirit of generous solidarity and sharing. No authentic human growth in peace and justice, in truth and freedom, can be achieved without the presence of Christ and his salvific power.

The building of a civilization of love requires strong and persevering characters, ready for self-sacrifice and anxious to open up new paths of human coexistence by overcoming divisions and the various forms of materialism. This is a responsibility of the young people of today who will be the men and women of tomorrow, at the dawn of the third Christian millennium.

In joyful anticipation of our meeting, I urge you all to undergo a deep and meditated spiritual preparation which may increase the ecclesial impetus of this World Day. Start out on the road! May your journey be marked by prayer, study, dialogue and the desire for conversion and a better life. Go forward united with each other in your parishes and Christian communities, in your associations and apostolic movements.

May yours be an attitude of acceptance and hope.

I send my affectionate and cordial greetings to all the young people of the world. I do so quite particularly to the young people of Argentina. I have followed with great interest your annual pilgrimages to the Sanctuary of Our Lady of Lujan and the National Youth Meeting held in Cordoba last year, as well as the "youth option" on which the overall pastoral ministry of the Argentine episcopate has for years been concentrated. Since my first visit to your country in 1982, so marked by suffering and hope, I have been familiar with your commitment to the building of peace in justice and truth. And through all this, I know that you are contributing with enthusiasm to the preparation of the World Day in Buenos Aires: that you will be present with the Pope at this meeting; and that you will be able to welcome with generous hospitality and shared friendship those young people from other countries who wish to participate in this celebration by pledging themselves to Christ, to the Church and to the new civilization of truth and love.

I urge all young men and women throughout the world to celebrate the Next World Day of Youth on Palm Sunday 1987 with particular intensity and hope. And I entrust its preparation and its fruits to Mary, the young Virgin of Nazareth, the humble servant of the Lord who believed in the love of the Father and gave us Christ, "our Peace" (cf. *Ephesians* 2:14).

Dear young people, my friends: be witnesses to the love of God, sowers of hope and builders of peace.

In the name of the Lord Jesus, I bless you with all my affection. (II WYD 1987)

And the Young People Reflect

Nicholas writes:

I have realized the more I fall in love with Christ, the more I will become like Him. The essence of WYD is to experience Christ and to deepen your relationship with Him. The truth of a powerful experience is most often reflected by how an individual changes from an experience, how they live out what he or she has learned. In the case of WYD, the truth of the power in the experience rests upon meeting Christ, encountering His love and then going home a changed person.

In some of the most trying situations, the hurt of a relationship or when I have a serious decision to make, I find myself drawn to the Eucharist. The Eucharist claims a high degree of transformation— the transformation of simple gifts of wheat and grapes into bread and wine which become the perfect sacrifice, Christ's body and blood. While most times when we digest food, the food becomes a part of us. Yet when we consume and eat Christ's body, we become more a part of Him. I have found myself, through this increased devotion to the Eucharist, transformed towards purity, peace and joy. Just as He promises, I find more "life" the more I participate in Mass. After Mass I sometimes stay to simply sit in His presence. The transformation that has taken place might have been best told by Saint Paul when he said, "I no longer live but Christ lives in me" (*Galatians* 2:20, NRSV). Through the Eucharist I become more like Him.

. . . and Melissa writes:

The Holy Father helped me to see the most important things of life, and he challenged me to be the witness I was intended to be. He expressed the reality that God was counting on me for this message to be transferred to others and to future generations. As a baptized Christian it was my duty and privilege. This was the test given to all of us that day, but for me, it was also a personal inspiration that I clung to in order to find out more about my vocation in life and how I would fulfill it in my own way.

Every pancake we flipped and served, every dinner plate we catered and every car we washed in order to travel to World Youth Day were all worth it. I had admired this man, John Paul II, for a long time. All that I had learned about him from my childhood, his fight to literally survive against the Nazis and Communism, his Polish heritage, his outreach to others, his desire to expel darkness and reveal the truth; I had admired it all, he was truly one of my heroes.

. . . and Andrei writes:

A friend of mine once told me, "How happy you are because you have the faith." That was true, but it did not mean that I would not have questions about my faith and even moments of despair, when I thought I did not believe any more. The world we live in is a permanent challenge to go beyond the evil and difficulties that surround us: we have not been "sentenced to life", a life of struggle and hardships without end. Life is a most precious gift, and being challenged to live it well only strengthens the one who does not give in.

I can only give thanks to God for the inestimable gift God gave the Church in the Holy Father! Who else gives such a testimony to the Truth, who else is willing to unmask evil and deceit and to point to the Good and Honest? Who else points out our true happiness, Jesus Christ?

. . . and Gottfried writes:

Back home in Austria I said to myself that I will never want to lose a World Youth Day and that I will tell as much people as possible about this great event!!!

. . . and Anthony writes:

There are many different challenges I face every day. For example, I use my walker to keep moving and to get my daily exercise because I want to walk again. My family and friends support me a lot. When I gave them the good news that I walked for three kilometers in one day, they were all very happy for me and made me feel good and said, "Keep up the good work." If I didn't have such caring friends and family members who have supported me in my every move, I don't know what I would do. For all of you out there who face the same challenges—never give up, you can do it. The choice is yours; make that step. There is more to life than being in a chair. You can do it. I know you can. It doesn't matter what religion you are, God will help you. Trust in Him and He will give you the strength you need. "For there shall be nothing impossible with God" (*Luke* 1:37).

. . . and Father Hernández writes:

There are no dividing lines in the church. We are a unique people of solidarity . . . composed of multiple groups with various cultures, sensibilities and diverse ways of acting in communion with the bishops, the pastors of the flock. This bond of our union is a sign of richness and of life.

. . . and Robert writes:

The morning before the Papal mass each group boarded their buses and began making their way out to the field. We had been told that it would be a one-mile walk to the field once we got off the bus. It turned out later on that this was supposed to be some sort of joke or morale booster or both. We continuously passed volunteers who held signs saying that we had just one more mile to go.

Santiago de Compostela, Spain
(15–20 August 1989)

Theme: "I Am the Way, the Truth and the Life" (*John* 14:6)

And so the Pope says:

Dear young people!

I am happy to be with you once again in order to announce the celebration of the IV World Youth Day. In my dialogue with you, this Day has, indeed, a privileged place. It affords me the welcome opportunity of speaking to the young people, not only of one country but of the whole world; of saying to each and every one of you that the Pope looks towards you with so much love and so much hope, that he listens to you with great attention and wishes to respond to your deepest aspirations.

World Youth Day 1989 will be centered on Jesus Christ, as our Way, our Truth and our Life (cf. *John* 14:6). For all of you it must therefore become the Day of a new, a more mature and a deeper discovery of Christ in your life.

To be young is already in itself a special and specific treasure for every young man and young woman (cf. "Letter to the Youth of the World," number 3). This treasure consists, among other things, in the fact that yours is an age of many important discoveries. Each one of you discovers his or her self, his or her personality, the meaning for him or for her of existence, the reality of good and evil. You also discover the whole world around you—the human world and the world of nature. Now, among these many discoveries there must not be lacking one that is of fundamental importance for every human being: *the personal discovery of Jesus Christ.* Discovering Christ, always again and always more fully, is the most wonderful adventure of our life. That is why, on the occasion of the forthcoming

Youth Day, I want to ask each one of you some very important questions, and to suggest the answers.

Have you already discovered Christ, who is the Way? Yes, Jesus is for us a way that leads to the Father—the only Way. You young people very often find yourselves at a crossroads, not knowing which path to choose, which way to go; there are so many wrong paths, so many facile proposals, so many ambiguities. In moments like this, do not forget that Christ, with his Gospel, his example, his commandments, is always and alone the safest way, the way which leads to full and lasting happiness.

Have you already discovered Christ, who is the Truth? Young people especially are hungry for the Truth about God and man, about life and the world. Truth is the deepest need of the human spirit. Christ is the Word of truth, uttered by God himself, in response to all the questioning of the human heart. He is the One who reveals fully to us the mystery . . . of the world.

Have you already discovered Christ, who is the Life? Each one of you is so anxious to live life in its fullness. You live with great hopes, with so many fine plans for the future. But do not forget that the true fullness of life is to be found only in Christ, who died and rose again for us. Christ alone is able to fill in depth the space of the human heart.

Yes, discovering Christ is the finest adventure of your life. But it is not enough to discover him just once. Discovering him becomes every time an invitation to seek him always more, to come to know him still better through prayer, participating in the sacraments, meditating on his Word, through catechesis and listening to the teachings of the Church. This is our most important task, as Saint Paul had well understood when he wrote: "For me, indeed, to live is Christ" (*Philippians* 1:21).

The new discovery of Christ—when it is authentic—always directly results in *the desire to bring him to others,* that is, in a commitment to the apostolate. This, precisely, is the second guideline for the next Youth Day.

To be Christians means to be missionaries, to be apostles (cf. *Apostolicam Actuositatem,* number 2). It is not enough to discover Christ—you must bring him to others!

The world of today is one great mission land, even in countries of long-standing Christian tradition. Everywhere today neopaganism and the process of secularization present *a great challenge to the message of the Gospel.* But, at the same time, there are new openings in our day for the proclamation of the Good News. We see, for example, a growing nostalgia for the sacred, for genuine values, for prayer. And so today's world needs many apostles—especially apostles who are young and courageous.

You young people have in a special way the task of witnessing today to the faith; the commitment to bring the Gospel of Christ—the Way, the Truth and the Life—into the third Christian Millennium, to build a new civilization—a civilization of love, of justice and of peace.

Each new generation needs new apostles. This means a special mission for you. You young people are the first apostles and evangelizers of the world of youth, assailed today by so many challenges and so much that is threatening (cf. *Apostolicam Actuositatem,* number 12). Above all, you can be evangelizers, and no one can take your place, where you study, and in your work and your free time. So many of those of our own age do not know Christ, or do not know him well enough. So you cannot remain silent and indifferent! You must have the courage to speak about Christ, to bear witness to your faith through a lifestyle inspired by the Gospel.

The harvest is great indeed for evangelization and so many workers are needed. Christ trusts you and counts on your collaboration. On the occasion of the forthcoming Youth Day, I invite you, therefore, to renew your apostolic commitment. Christ needs you! Respond to his call with courage and with the enthusiasm that belongs to your age.

The famous Sanctuary of Santiago de Compostela, in Spain, will be a very important point of reference for the celebration of this Day in 1989. As I have already told you, after the ordinary celebration of your feast—Palm Sunday—in the particular Churches, I give you a rendezvous at that Sanctuary; I will go there, a pilgrim like yourselves, for the 19th and 20th of August. I am sure you will not fail to respond to my invitation, as you did not fail for the unforgettable meeting in Buenos Aires, in 1987.

The appointment at Santiago will in any case be a moment of participation for the whole of the Universal Church; a moment of spiritual communion even for those among you who will not be able to be physically present. At Santiago the young people will indeed represent the particular Churches of the whole world; you will all be heirs to the "Santiago Trail" with the urge to proclaim the Good News.

Santiago de Compostela is a place that has played a very important role in the history of Christianity; and, so, its spiritual message is in itself very eloquent.

At the tomb of Saint James we want to learn that our faith has historical foundations; it is not something vague and transient. In the world of today, marked by a serious relativism and great confusion in values, we must always remember that, as

Christians, we are truly built up on the stable foundations of the Apostles, with Christ himself as the cornerstone (cf. *Ephesians* 2:20).

Santiago de Compostela is not only a Sanctuary. It is also a route: a closely-woven network of pilgrimage roads. The "Santiago Trail" was for centuries a pathway to conversion and an extraordinary witness to faith. Along this way arose visible monuments to the pilgrims' faith: churches and hospices.

Pilgrimage has a very deep spiritual significance; it can represent in itself an important form of catechesis. The Church—as the Second Vatican Council reminded us—is, indeed, a people of God on the march, "in search of a future and permanent city" (cf. *Lumen Gentium*, number 9).

In the world today there is a revival of the practice of going on pilgrimage, especially among the youth. Today, you are among those more inclined to experience a pilgrimage as a "way" to interior renewal, to a deepening of faith, a strengthening of the sense of communion and solidarity with your brothers and sisters and as a help in discovering your personal vocation.

The programme of this Day is very demanding. To gather its fruits you will therefore need a specific spiritual preparation, under the guidance of your pastors, in your dioceses, parishes, associations and movements. This will be necessary both for Palm Sunday and for the pilgrimage to Santiago de Compostela in August 1989. At the beginning of this preparatory phase, I address to each and every one of you the words of the Apostle Paul: "Walk in love . . . ; walk as children of light" (*Ephesians* 5:2,8). Enter upon this period of preparation with these dispositions.

Be on your way, then, I say to all of you, young pilgrims of the "Santiago Trail". During the pilgrimage days, try to recapture the spirit of the pilgrims of old, courageous witnesses to the Christian faith. As you journey on, learn to discover Jesus, who is our Way, Truth and Life.

Finally, I want to address a special word of encouragement to the young people of Spain. This time it will be for you to offer hospitality to your brothers and sisters from all over the world. It is my wish for you that this meeting at Santiago may leave deep traces in your life and may be for all of you a powerful leaven of spiritual renewal.

Dear young people, this Message of mine ends with an embrace of peace which I want to extend to all of you, wherever you may be. I entrust the ongoing preparation and the celebration of the World Youth Day 1989 to the special protection of Mary, Queen of Apostles, and of Saint James who, throughout the centuries, has been venerated at the ancient Sanctuary of Compostela. May my Apostolic Blessing—as a sign of encouragement and good wishes—accompany you all along your route.
(IV WYD 1989)

And the Young People Reflect

Nicholas writes:

Many people often cite their most powerful experience of WYD as seeing the Holy Father. While this certainly was an unforgettable moment for me, there were other deeply profound moments of grace throughout the week. One such event occurred at the Opening Ceremony where my group and I had about a seven-hour wait for the Holy Father to arrive. We were hot, sweaty and tired; there was no shade and we did not have much food either. We were cramped. We desperately tried to save ourselves room by spreading out our bags, but we quickly rubbed elbows with others. And after we were already squeezed together, an announcement was made to move even closer to accommodate more people. Sacrifice was a key lesson I learned, and the comment that so many people make on pilgrimages is true: "This is a pilgrimage, not a vacation. There will be sacrifices." And compared to what we were used to, we did sacrifice. Yet God will not be outdone in generosity. He will reward us for our sacrifices.

. . . and Gottfried writes:

I still see the Pope standing on the big stage and hear him preaching to us. The Pope spoke right into my heart. At this time I felt my weakness and knew about my young age . . . but the Pope spoke right against my doubts. He encouraged us to go out and preach the Gospel! At that time I would have never thought about what happened in my life, but I felt that the Lord was calling me through our Pope John Paul II! This was a very special feeling for me which I experienced the first time in my life in such a special way!

. . . and Charles writes:

We, the young people in Kenya, Africa, are faced by many gigantic problems. In all sincerity and honesty, life is a misery here. Just mention any life-threateing problem in any part of the world and you can surely find it in Africa. For example, drug abuse, child soldiers, child labour, marriage of young girls to older men, unemployment, tribal and civil wars, diseases (especially HIV-AIDS), illiteracy, poverty, severe famines and droughts, dictatorship from our political leaders who overthrow people-elected governments, lack of role models and many more. The Pope and the UN have changed our lives completely for they have heard our sobbing.

. . . and Melissa writes:

The crowds, the sun, the language barrier, all contributed to a truly challenging pilgrimage. Truthfully, these are the things I remember most. For me, it was a time to minister to my peers, to comfort them in their stress and try hard to see Christ in all that was happening around me.

The Holy Father, though at a distance, I believe, understood some of this hardship. He realized the sacrifice we had made to travel and spend the night outside waiting for his arrival. This was evident to me when after driving around a bit in the pope mobile along the aisles, I heard the translator say, "He is motioning the driver to go further back." Instead of stopping, he wanted to satisfy some of the youth way in the back by, at least, giving them a wave and a closer sighting of his presence among them. He was not a movie star looking for attention, but a father seeking out his children. Though aging and probably tired himself, he wanted the youth to know that he loved them all and he was here for them.

Czestochowa, Poland
(10—15 August 1991)

Theme: "You have received a spirit of sonship" (*Romans* 8:15).

And so the Pope says:

Dear young people!

The World Youth Days mark important stages in the life of the Church, as she seeks to intensify her commitment to evangelization in today's world, looking towards the year 2000. By proposing every year for your meditation *certain essential truths* of the Gospel teaching, these Days are intended to give nourishment for your faith and new energies for your apostolate.

As the theme of the Sixth World Youth Day, I have chosen the words of Saint Paul: "*You have received a spirit of sonship*" (*Romans* 8:15). These words lead us into the deepest mystery of the Christian vocation: in the divine plan, we are indeed called to become *sons and daughters of God in Christ, through the Holy Spirit.*

How can we fail to be amazed at the heights to which we are called? The human being—a created and limited being, even a sinner—is destined to be a child of God! How can we fail to exclaim with Saint John: "See what love the Father has given us, that we should be called children of God; and so we are!" (*1 John* 3:1)? How can we remain indifferent to this challenge of God's paternal love, inviting us to so deep and intimate a communion?

As you celebrate the next World Day, let this holy amazement take possession of you, inspiring in each one of you an ever more filial attachment to God, our Father.

"*You have received a spirit of sonship* . . ." The Holy Spirit, the true agent of our divine sonship, has regenerated us to new life in the waters of Baptism.

From that moment, he "bears witness with our spirit that we are children of God" (*Romans* 8:16).

What does it mean, in the life of the Christian, to be a son or daughter of God: Saint Paul writes: "All who are led by the Spirit of God are sons of God" (*Romans* 8:14). To be sons and daughters of God means, therefore, to receive the Holy Spirit, to let ourselves be guided by him, to be open to his action in our personal history and in the history of the world.

To all of you young people, on the occasion of this World Youth Day, I say: *Receive the Holy Spirit and be strong in faith!* "God did not give us a spirit of timidity but a spirit of power and love and self-control" (*2 Timothy* 1:7).

I am thinking of the profound changes taking place in the world. For many peoples the doors are opening the hope of a life more worthy of them and more human. In this connection, I recall the truly prophetic words of the Second Vatican Council: "The Spirit of God, who with marvellous providence directs the course of history and renews the face of the earth, is present in this evolution" (*Gaudium et spes*, number 26).

Yes, *the Spirit of the sons and daughters of God is the driving force in the history of peoples.* In every age, the Spirit raises up new men and women who live in holiness, in truth and in justice. On the threshold of the year 2000, the world that is anxiously seeking ways of living together in greater solidarity urgently needs to count on persons who, with the help of the Holy Spirit, are capable of living as true children of God.

Saint Paul speaks to us of the *heritage of the sons and daughters of God.* What is meant is a gift of eternal life, but at the same time, a task to be carried out already today, a design for life that is fascinating, especially for you young people, who, in your inmost hearts, have a yearning for high ideals.

Holiness is the essential heritage of the children of God. Christ says: "Be perfect, as your heavenly Father is perfect" (*Matthew* 5:48). This means doing the will of the Father in every circumstance of life. It is the high road that Jesus has pointed out to us: "Not every one who says to me, 'Lord, Lord', shall enter the kingdom of heaven, but he who does the will of my Father who is in heaven" (*Matthew* 7:21).

I repeat again today what I said at Santiago de Compostela: "*Young people, do not be afraid to be holy!*" Fly high, be among those whose goals are worthy of sons and daughters of God. Glorify God in your lives!

"Love one another, as I have loved you" (*John* 15:12). If we call upon God as "Father", we cannot fail to recognize in our neighbour—whoever this may be—a brother or sister who has a right to our love. This is the great commitment for the children of God: working to build a society in which all peoples will live fraternally together.

Is not this what the world most needs today? Within nations we can feel the strength of longing for unity that will break down every barrier of indifference and hate. It is especially for you, young people, to take on the great task of *building a society where there will be more justice and solidarity.*

Another prerogative of the children of God is freedom; this also is part of their heritage. We touch here on a subject to which you young people are particularly sensitive, because what is at issue is an immense gift that the Creator has placed in our hands. But a gift that must be used rightly. How many *false forms of freedom* there are, leading to slavery!

In the Encyclical *Redemptor Hominis* I wrote on this subject: "Jesus Christ meets the men and women of every age, including our own, with the same words: 'You will know the truth and the truth will make you free' (*John* 8:32). These words contain both a fundamental requirement and a warning: the requirement of an honest relationship to truth as a condition for authentic freedom, and the warning to avoid every kind of illusory freedom, every superficial unilateral freedom, every freedom that fails to enter into the whole truth about the human being and the world. Today also, even after two thousand years, we see Christ as the one who brings men and women freedom based on truth . . ." (number 12).

"When Christ freed us he meant us to remain free" (*Galatians* 5:1). Liberation by Christ is liberation from sin, the root of all human slaveries. Saint Paul says: "You who were once slaves of sin have become obedient from the heart to the standard of teaching to which you were committed, and, having been set free from sin, have become slaves of righteousness" (*Romans* 6:17). Freedom, therefore, is a gift and, at the same time, an essential duty for every Christian: "You did not receive the spirit of slavery . . ." (*Romans* 8:15), the Apostle reminds us.

Exterior freedom, guaranteed by just civil laws, is important and necessary. We rightly rejoice that today, in an ever increasing number of countries, the fundamental rights of the human person are respected, even if, not infrequently, there has been a high price to pay in sacrifice and bloodshed. But, however precious, exterior freedom alone is not enough. It must be rooted always in the interior freedom that belongs to the children of God, who live according to the Spirit (cf. *Galatians* 5:16) and are guided by an upright moral conscience, capable of choosing what is truly good. "Where the Spirit of the Lord is, there is freedom" (*2 Corinthians* 3:17). This, dear young people, is the only path to take if humankind is to become mature and worthy of its name.

See, then, how great and challenging is *the heritage of the sons and daughters of God*, to which you are called. Receive it with gratitude and responsibility. Do not waste it! Have the courage, every day, to live by it consistently and to announce it to others. In this way, the world will become, more and more, *the great family of the sons and daughters of God.*

At the heart of the World Youth Day 1991 there will be another *world youth rally.*

This time, to conclude the customary meetings and celebrations in the dioceses, we will meet to pray together at the Shrine of Our Lady of Czestochowa, in Poland, my home country. Many of you, remembering the experience of the pilgrimage to Santiago de Compostela (1989), will flock joyfully to this rendezvous on the Feast of the Assumption of the Blessed Virgin Mary, 14 and 15 August 1991. In our hearts and in our prayers, we will bring with us the youth of the whole world.

Set out therefore, already now, on your way to the dwelling of the Mother of Christ and our Mother, meditating, under her loving gaze, on the theme of the Sixth World Day: *"You have received a spirit of sonship . . ."*

Where better than at the feet of God's Mother can we learn what it means to be sons and daughters of God? Mary is the best teacher. The role entrusted to her was fundamental for the history of salvation.

Where better than in her maternal heart can we guard the heritage of the sons and daughters of God Promised by the Father? We bear this gift in vessels of clay. For each one of us, our pilgrimage will be, therefore, a great act of entrustment to Mary. We will be going to a Shrine which, for the Polish people, has a very special significance as a place of evangelization and conversion; a Shrine to which thousands of pilgrims make their way from all parts of the country and of the world.

For more than 600 years, in the Monastery of Jasna Góra at Czestochowa, Mary has been venerated in the miraculous icon of the Black Madonna. There, at the most difficult moments of its history, the Polish people has found, in the Mother's house, the strength of faith and hope, its own dignity and the heritage of the children of God.

For the young people of East and West, of North and South, for all, the pilgrimage to Czestochowa will be a witness of faith to the whole world. It will be a pilgrimage of freedom across the frontiers of States which, more and more, are opening to Christ, Redeemer of humanity.

My intention with this Message is to inaugurate the journey of spiritual preparation both for the Sixth World Youth Day and for the pilgrimage to Czestochowa. These reflections are meant to serve as initial steps on this journey, which is above all one of faith, of conversion and of a return to the essentials of our life.

For you, young people of the countries of Eastern Europe, I have a word of special encouragement. Do not miss this appointment. Already now, it can be seen as a memorable encounter between the youth of the Churches of East and West. Your presence at Czestochowa will be an immensely meaningful witness to faith.

And you, dear young people of my beloved Poland, you are called this time to give hospitality to your friends from all parts of the world. For you and for the Church of Poland this encounter, in which I too will take part, will be an extraordinary spiritual gift at this moment of your history, so full of hope for the future.

Kneeling in spirit before the image of the Black Madonna of Czestochowa, I entrust to her loving protection the whole event of the Sixth World Youth Day.

For you, dear young people, my warm paternal Blessing. (VI WYD 1991)

And the Young People Reflect

Andrei writes:

That vigil was one of the most precious moments with the Holy Father I had ever had. There were a few words which he repeated over and over again during his homily which touched me particularly: *"laboratorio della fede"* (laboratory of faith). That was what the Apostles experienced, that was what we were called to.

. . . and Charles writes:

I say Kudos to our beloved Pope. He may not know, but he has touched my life though he is very far from where I live. I love him. Long live Papa! For sure, I am still doing my studies as I discern my vocation. I take time to listen to God so that I can know what he wants with my life. And after everything is said and done, I am sure of one thing, that I am always prepared to "make a defence to any one who calls me to account for the hope that is in me" (*1 Peter* 3:15, NRSV).

. . . and Melissa writes:

Mass with the Holy Father was, of course, the highlight of the trip. To see so many Catholic young people from so many different countries and cultures gathered in one place and united by one faith was truly amazing. Though the culture and language was a roadblock in one way, on the other hand, it was also a vibrant example of how Christ could unite so many people from so many different walks of life. In our heads, we prayed in different languages, but said the same prayer. In our ears, we heard all the foreign words and accents but when translated into our own tongue, we understood the same message. Each culture presented itself to the Holy Father by a different dance or expression, but we all saw the same love represented in their hearts. It was here that my love for culture and the individuality of each and every person on the earth began to develop. Though many moments were weary, I saw the same strong desire, the same real fire within every other human heart to be loved and to love. This mystery is one, which the Holy Father understood so well, not just because he was a caring man but because he had taken Christ into the depth of his being and committed himself to the Christian way of life, a life that meant seeking out the hungry and the lost and then, loving each one with dignity.

. . . and Nicholas writes:

While the gathering of two million individuals is amazing but perhaps more daunting when one considers the power of God. The crowds would span further than I could see. One of the individuals I traveled with, Keith (now Father Keith), commented that it is amazing to see the crowd and think that

God knows each person intimately. He can count the hairs on their head and hear all their prayers at the same time. Seeing the huge crowd and knowing how close God is to each person brought about a deep awe of the Lord as well as a sense of His compassion to give Himself to each person.

. . . and Gottfried writes:

I still remember the long walk to the big field where we stayed for the Vigil and the ending Mass. Just some time before the Pope was going to come, it started to rain. Me and my friend went through the crowd of people, closer to the stage, and we saw the full cloudy sky and we started to pray the rosary.

. . . and Gail writes:

What a thrill to be so close to someone like the Pope and to be able to watch young people sing, chant, dance, and pray with such love and respect for a man. To watch a frail, yet strong man love and respect each of these young people was something I will never forget. He was one of them, maybe not in body, but definitely in faith and love for the Catholic Church. His spirit never faltered in each of the speeches that he gave these pilgrims, and their respect for him never diminished.

Denver, United States
(10–15 August 1993)

Theme: "I came that they may have life, and have it to the full"
(*John* 10:10).

And so the Pope says:

Dear Young People,

Following our meetings in Rome, Buenos Aires, Santiago de Compostela and Czestochowa, our pilgrimage through contemporary history continues. The next stop will be in Denver, in the heart of the United States, in the Rocky Mountains of Colorado, where in August 1993 the Eighth World Youth Day will be celebrated. Together with many young Americans, young people from every nation will gather together, as on previous occasions, as if to symbolize the living faith, or at least the most urgent questionings of the world of youth from the five continents.

These regular celebrations are not meant to be *mere rituals*, justified merely by the fact that they are repeated; in fact, they spring from a *deep-seated need* originating in the human heart and reflected in the life of the pilgrim and missionary Church.

The World Youth Days and Gatherings are *providential opportunities to break our journey for a while*: they enable young people to examine their deepest aspirations, to heighten their sense of be-longing to the Church, to proclaim their common faith in the crucified and risen Christ with increasing joy and courage. They provide an opportunity for many young people to make bold and enlightened choices which can help steer the future course of history under the powerful but gentle guidance of the Holy Spirit.

We are witnessing a "succession of empires" in our world—the repeated attempts to create political unity which particular individuals have tried to impose on others. The results are there for all to see. True and lasting unity cannot be created by coercion and violence. It can be achieved only by building on the foundations of a common heritage of values accepted and shared by all, values such as respect for the dignity of the human person, a willingness to welcome life, the defence of human rights, and openness to transcendence and the realm of the spirit.

In view of this, and as a response to the challenges of our changing times, the World Youth Gathering is meant to be a *first step and a proposal of a new unity*, a unity which transcends the political order but enlightens it. It is based on awareness that only the Creator of the human heart can adequately satisfy its deepest yearnings. World Youth Day is thus a proclamation of Christ who says to the men and women of our own century too: "I came that they might have life, and have it to the full" (*John* 10:10).

There is no better word than 'life" to sum up comprehensively the greatest aspiration of all humanity. "Life" indicates the sum total of all the goods that people desire, and at the same time what makes them possible, obtainable and lasting.

Human existence has its moments of crisis and weariness, despondency and gloom. Such a sense of dissatisfaction is clearly reflected in much of today's literature and films. In the light of this distress, it is easier to understand the particular difficulties of adolescents and young people stepping out with uncertainty to encounter all the fascinating promises and dark uncertainties which are part of life.

Jesus came to provide the ultimate answer to the yearning for life and for the infinite which his Heavenly Father had poured into our hearts when he created us. At the climax of revelation, the incarnate Word proclaims, "I am the Life" (*John* 14:6), and "I came that they might have life" (*John* 10:10). But what life? Jesus' intention was clear: *the very life of God*, which surpasses all the possible aspirations of the human heart (cf. *1 Corinthians* 2:9). The fact is that through the grace of Baptism we are already God's children (cf. *1 John* 3:1–2).

Jesus came to meet men and women, to heal the sick and the suffering, to free those possessed by devils and to raise the dead: he gave himself on the cross and rose again from the dead, revealing that he is *the Lord of life*: the author and the source of life without end.

Our daily experience tells us that life is marked by sin and threatened by *death*, despite the desire for good which beats in our hearts and the desire for life which courses through our veins. However little heed we pay to ourselves and to the frustrations which life brings us, we discover that *everything within us impels us to transcend ourselves*, urges us to overcome the temptation of superficiality or despair. It is then that human beings are called to become disciples of that other One who infinitely transcends them, in order to enter at last into true life.

There are also *false prophets* and *false teachers of how to live*. First of all there are those who teach people to leave the body, time and space in order to be able to enter into what they call "true life". They condemn creation, and in the name of deceptive spirituality they lead thousands of young people along the paths of an impossible liberation which eventually leaves them even more isolated, victims of their own illusions and of the evil in their own lives.

Seemingly at the opposite extreme, there are the teachers of the "fleeting moment", who invite people to give free rein to every instinctive urge or longing, with the result that individuals fall prey to a sense of anguish and anxiety leading them to seek refuge in false, artificial paradises, such as that of drugs.

There are also those who teach that the meaning of life lies solely in the quest for success, the accumulation of wealth, the development of personal abilities, without regard for the needs of others or respect for values, at times not even for the fundamental value of life itself.

These and other kinds of false teachers of life, also numerous in the modern world, propose goals which not only fail to bring satisfaction but often intensify and exacerbate the thirst that burns in the human heart.

Who then can understand and satisfy our expectations? Who but the One who is the Author of Life can satisfy the expectations that he himself has placed in our hearts? He draws close to each and every one of us in order to announce a hope that will never disappoint; he who is both the way and the life: *the pathway into life.*

In the mystery of his cross and resurrection, Christ has destroyed death and sin, and has bridged the infinite distance that separates all people from new life in him. "I am the resurrection and the life", he proclaims. "Whoever believes in me, though he should die, will come to life, and whoever is alive and believes in me will never die" (*John* 11:25).

Christ achieves all this by pouring out his Spirit, the giver of life, *in the sacraments*; especially in *Baptism*, the sacrament by which the fragile life which we receive from our parents and which is destined to end in death becomes instead a path to eternity; in the sacrament of *Penance* which continually renews God's life within us by the forgiveness of sins; and in the *Eucharist*, the "bread of life" (cf. *John* 6:34), which feeds the "living" and gives strength to their steps during their pilgrimage on earth, so that they can say with the Apostle Paul: "I still live my human life, but it is a life of faith in the Son of God who loved me and gave himself for me".

That new life begins to flower here and now. The sign of its presence and growth is love. As Saint John tells us: "That we have passed from death to life we know because we love the brothers" (*1 John* 3:14) with a true love that is put into practice. Life flourishes in the gift of self to others, in accordance with each person's vocation—in the ministerial priesthood, in consecrated virginity, in marriage—so that all can share the gifts they have received, in a spirit of solidarity, especially with the poor and the needy.

You can find the answer by yourselves, if you really try to live faithfully in the love of Christ (cf. *John* 15:9). Then you will personally experience the truth of those words of his: "I am . . . the life" (*John* 14:6) and you will be able to bring this joyful message of hope to everyone. Christ has made you his ambassadors, the primary evangelizers of your contemporaries.

The next World Youth Day in Denver will give us an ideal opportunity to reflect together on this theme of great interest to everyone. We must therefore prepare for this important meeting, first of all by looking around us to discover and, make a list, as it were, of all the "places" where Christ is present as the source of life. They may be our parish communities, apostolic groups and movements, monasteries, convents and religious houses, but also the individual persons through whom—as the disciples at Emmaus experienced—Christ is able to touch hearts and open them up to hope.

You, *dear young people of the United States* who will be the hosts of the next World Youth Day, have been given the joy of welcoming as a gift of the Spirit this meeting with the many young men and women who will come to your country on pilgrimage from all over the world.

You are already making fervent spiritual and material preparations for this event, which involves each member of your ecclesial communities.

It is my earnest hope that this extraordinary event will bring you ever greater enthusiasm and fidelity in following Christ and in joyfully welcoming his message, the source of new life.

I therefore entrust all of you to the Blessed Virgin Mary, through whom we have been given the Author of Life, Jesus Christ, the Son of God and our Lord. With great affection I send all of you my blessing. (VIII WYD 1993)

And the Young People Reflect

Gottfried writes:

Now was the time we started with many other buses the trip to Denver! To see so many buses filled with young people was a great feeling for me! Especially how they treated each other. I still remember a young handicapped lady, who was working at a fast-food restaurant on the way to Denver. First I was touched to see how the other workers were dealing with her, and when I was close to her, she asked me what we are doing here and where we are going to. So we talked about the World Youth Day, and she told me that she would be so happy to come with us; but she couldn't go, so she asked us to pray for her. So I took her with me in my prayers!

. . . and Paul writes:

Looking back on the Holy Father's celebration of WYD '93 in the United States, many people believe that this gathering was a tremendous event for the entire church in the U.S. For young people, it was a moment to be proud of their faith, to publicly demonstrate their faith. It was a moment to realize that as a Catholic, they were part of a community much larger than their parish or even diocese. Standing on the hillside, looking down at 300,000 other young people, you knew you were part of something bigger than yourself.

For the bishops, some of them have described it as a moment of awareness of the potential and power of youth and ministry with young people. So many bishops left Denver saying how the event energized their own ministry and intensified their understanding of ministry with youth. One bishop even described WYD as a moment in time when young people themselves evangelized the bishops!

. . . and Robert writes:

When Ann Cronin, our youth minister, asked who wanted to go to Denver, Colorado, to see the Pope, I think my first question was why Denver and not the Vatican? It was during our preparation for World Youth Day that we discovered the fact that the Pope had been traveling the world every two years in the summer months for the sole purpose of meeting with his Catholic youth from around the world.

The morning sun is what I remember most from that entire week we spent in Denver. Maybe it was the altitude or the attitude, I don't know if I will ever know. What I do know is that moment, that day, that World Youth Day changed the course of my life forever.

I have come to find out that it is a World Youth Day tradition to wake us at sunrise with the theme song for that year. This was no different as "We Are One Body" came blasting out of the huge speakers surrounding the field. Thousands of voices joined in as people began getting breakfast prepared, making water runs, and getting sleeping bags re-rolled. There was a charge in the air as we all eagerly awaited the arrival of the Holy Father. This was it, the moment we had prepared for, starting two years before, back in our parish. This was the purpose of our eight-mile hike that we had undertaken to bring us to this field. The moment we saw the three Blackhawk helicopters approaching the field and then touching down some distance away, the huge video screens began showing live feed from the television cameras flying overhead. You could feel the electricity and excitement in the air, as hundreds of thousands of young people from around the world awaited the arrival of our spiritual father, Pope John Paul II.

. . . and Melissa writes:

With those last remarks, he received arousing applause and the familiar chant of love for him began: "John Paul II, we love you! John Paul II, we love you!"

Just as the disciples in the Scriptures, we, as young people, were ready to follow Christ also. We expressed our love for Him by chanting our love for John Paul II, God's servant on earth and our mentor and guide. John Paul II invested in us, the Church of the future and the Church of that very moment. He did not sugarcoat the hardships of life and in fact pointed out the reality of the journey toward the cross as Christians. He revealed for us the depth of Christ's love in his own flesh and with his words of truth. He challenged us and trusted us; he did not assume we were incapable or immature like so many others had.

. . . and Father Hernandez writes:

Baptism and Confirmation do not take us from the world, but through them we share the joys and hopes of all peoples and we offer our contribution to the human community in the social aspects of life, and in the technical and scientific field also. Thanks to Christ we are near all our brothers and sisters, in order to shine forth with profound joy which has in it, living with Christ. The Lord calls us to accomplish our mission of joy right where we are because the place where God has placed us is so beautiful that we are never permitted to desert Him.

. . . and Andrei writes:

When the Pope came, the youth gathered in the square would not stop cheering, "JP II, we love you!" I don't remember everything the Pope said then, but I remember that the pavement stones in the square were so hot that one could not sit on them. There was a gigantic water hose sprinkling the youth in the square, and we longed so much for a little water. All those young people, from all over the world, gathered there to listen to the Pope! It was very impressive! I didn't think of this then, but my peers there seemed more interested in the water coming from the Holy Father's words than in the actual water from the hose.

Manila, Philippines
(10—15 January 1995)

Theme: "As the Father sent me, so I am sending you" (*John* 20:21).

And so the Pope says:

> *Dear Young People,*
> "Peace be with you!" (*John* 20:19). This is the greeting, rich in meaning, which the risen Lord extended to the disciples, so fearful and dismayed after his passion.
> With the same intense and deep feeling I now address you, as we prepare to celebrate the Ninth and Tenth World Youth Days. They will take place, as is now the pleasant custom, on Palm Sunday of 1994 and 1995, while the great international meeting, which gathers young people from all over the world around the Pope, is set for January 1995 in Manila, capital of the Philippines.
> In the previous meetings that have marked our journey of reflection and prayer, like the disciples, we have had the opportunity of "seeing"—which also means believing and knowing, almost "touching" (cf. *1 John* 1:1)—the risen Lord.
> We "saw" him and welcomed him as teacher and friend in Rome in 1984 and 1985, when we began our pilgrimage from the centre and heart of Catholicism in order to give a reason for the hope that is in us (cf. *1 Peter* 3:15), carrying his cross along the highways of the world. We asked him—insistently— to be with us in our daily journey.
> We "saw" him in Buenos Aires in 1987 when, together with the young people of every continent, especially from Latin America, "we came to know and believe in the love God has for us" (*1 John* 4:16) and we proclaimed that his revelation, like the sun that sheds light and warmth, nourishes the hope and

renews the joy of the missionary commitment to build the civilization of love.

We "saw" him in Santiago de Compostela in 1988, where we discovered his face and recognized him as *the way and the truth and the life* (*John* 14:6), while together with the Apostle James we meditated on the ancient Christian roots of Europe.

We "saw" him in 1991 in Czestochowa, when—with barriers fallen—all together, young people from East and West, under the kindly gaze of our heavenly Mother, we proclaimed the fatherhood of God through the Spirit and we acknowledged that we are—in him—brothers and sisters: "You received a spirit of adoption" (*Romans* 8:15).

Man is driven to seek the face of God

Recently we "saw" him again in Denver, in the heart of the United States of America, where we sought him in the face of contemporary man in a substantially different context from the previous pauses, but no less exalting for the depth of its significance, experiencing and tasting the gift of life in abundance: "I came that they might have life and have it more abundantly" (*John* 10:10).

As we keep before our eyes and in our hearts the wonderful and unforgettable spectacle of that great meeting in the Rocky Mountains, our pilgrimage continues and this time pauses in Manila, in the vast continent of Asia, the crossroads of the Tenth World Youth Day.

Once again, young people from all over the world are summoned by Jesus Christ, the centre of our lives, the basis of our faith, the reason for our hope and the source of our charity.

Called by him, young people from every corner of the globe ask themselves about their commitment to the "new evangelization", continuing the mission entrusted to the Apostles and in which every

Christian, through his Baptism and membership in the community of the Church, is called to participate.

The vocation and missionary commitment of the Church spring from the central mystery of our faith: Easter. It is in fact "on the evening of that first day" that Jesus appeared to the disciples, barricaded behind locked doors "for fear of the Jews" (*John* 20:19).

We hope to triumph in the fullness of time

Having given proof of his boundless love by embracing the cross and offering himself in sacrifice for the redemption of all people—he had in fact said: "No one has greater love than this, to lay down one's life for one's friends" (*John* 15:13)—the divine Master returns among his own, among those whom he had loved most intensely and with whom he had spent his earthly life.

It is an extraordinary encounter, during which their hearts are filled with happiness for the refound presence of Christ, after the events of his tragic passion and his glorious resurrection. The disciples "rejoiced when they saw the Lord" (*John* 20:20).

Meeting him on the day after his resurrection meant for the Apostles that they could see with their own eyes that his message was not false, that his promises were not written in the sand. He, alive and blazing with glory, is the proof of the almighty love of God, which radically changes the course of history and of our individual lives.

The meeting with Jesus is therefore the event which gives meaning to human life and profoundly alters it, by opening the spirit to horizons of authentic freedom.

Our time too occurs "on the day after the resurrection". It is "the acceptable time", "the day of salvation" (2 *Corinthians* 6:2).

The risen Christ returns among us with the fullness of joy and with overflowing richness of life. Hope becomes certainty, because if he has conquered death, we too can hope to triumph one day in the fullness of time, in the period of the final contemplation of God.

However the meeting with the risen Lord does not reflect only a moment of personal joy. It is rather the occasion when the call that awaits every human being is shown in all its breadth. Strong in our faith in the risen Christ, we are all invited to open the doors of life, without fear or doubt, to welcome the Word which is the Way, the Truth and the Life (cf. *John* 14:6), and to shout it courageously to the whole world.

The salvation offered to us is a gift that should not be jealously hidden. It is like the light of the sun, which by its nature breaks through the darkness; it is like the water of a clear spring, which gushes from the heart of the rock.

"God so loved the world that he gave his only Son" (*John* 3:16). Jesus, sent by the Father to mankind, communicates the abundance of life to every believer (cf. *John* 10:10), as we reflected and proclaimed on the occasion of the recent Day in Denver.

His Gospel must become "communication" and mission. The missionary vocation summons every Christian; it becomes the very essence of every testimony of concrete and living faith. It is a mission which traces its origins from the Father's plan, the plan of love and salvation which is carried out through the power of the Spirit, without which every apostolic initiative is destined to failure. It is to enable his disciples to carry out this mission that Jesus says to them: "Receive the Holy Spirit" (*John* 20:22). He thus transmits to the Church his own saving mission, so that the Easter mystery may

continue to be communicated to every person, in every age, in every corner of the globe.

You, young people, are especially called to become missionaries of this New Evangelization, by daily witnessing to the Word that saves.

You personally experience the anxieties of the present historical period, fraught with hope and doubt, in which it can at times be easy to lose the way that leads to the encounter with Christ.

In fact, numerous are the temptations of our time, the seductions that seek to muffle the divine voice resounding within the heart of each individual.

We are sent to proclaim hope and reconciliation

To the people of our century, to all of you, dear young people, who hunger and thirst for truth, the Church offers herself as a travelling companion. She offers the eternal Gospel message and entrusts you with an exalting apostolic task: to be the protagonists of the New Evangelization.

As the faithful guardian and representative of the wealth of faith transmitted to her by Christ, she is ready to enter into dialogue with the new generations; in order to answer their needs and expectations and to find in frank and open dialogue the most appropriate way to reach the source of divine salvation.

The Church entrusts to young people the task of proclaiming to the world the joy which springs from having met Christ. Dear friends, allow yourselves to be drawn to Christ; accept his invitation and follow him. Go and preach the Good News that redeems (cf. *Matthew* 28:19); do it with happiness in your hearts and become *communicators of hope* in a world which is often tempted to despair, *communicators of faith* in a society which at times seems resigned to disbelief, *communicators of love* in daily events that are often marked by a mentality of the most unbridled selfishness.

Each one of you is sent into the world, especially among your contemporaries, to communicate through the example of your life and work the Gospel message of reconciliation and peace: "We implore you on behalf of Christ, be reconciled to God" (2 *Corinthians* 5:20).

This reconciliation is in the first place the individual destiny of every Christian who receives and continuously renews his personal identity as a disciple of the Son of God in prayer and through receiving the sacraments, especially Penance and the Eucharist.

But it is also the destiny of the whole human family. To be a missionary today in the heart of our society also means making the best use of the media for that religious and pastoral task.

Having become enthusiastic communicators of the saving Word and witnesses to the joy of Easter, you will be builders of peace in a world that searches for this peace as if for a utopia, often forgetting its origin. Peace—as you well know—resides in the heart of every man, if only he knows how to open himself to the greeting of the risen Redeemer: "Peace be with you" (*John* 20:19).

In view of the imminent arrival of the third Christian millennium, to you young people the task of becoming communicators of hope and peacemakers is entrusted in a special way (cf. *Matthew* 5:9) in a world that is ever more in need of credible witnesses and consistent messengers. Know how to speak to the hearts of your contemporaries, who thirst for truth and happiness, in a constant, even if often unconscious, search for God.

Dear young people of the whole world!

As the journey towards the Ninth and Tenth World Youth Days officially begins with this Message, I wish again to express my affectionate greeting to each one of you, especially to all who live in the Philippines: in 1995 the world meeting of young people with the Pope will be celebrated for the first time on the Asian continent, so rich in tradition and culture.

Young people of the Philippines, it is your turn to prepare a welcome for your many friends from all over the world. So, the young Church of Asia is called in a special way to give a lively and vibrant testimony of faith at the appointment in Manila. My wish is that she will know how to receive this gift that Christ himself is about to offer her.

To you all, young people from every part of the world, I extend my invitation to journey in spirit towards the next Youth Days. Accompanied and guided by your Pastors, in your parishes and Dioceses, in the ecclesial associations, movements and groups, be ready to receive the seeds of holiness and grace which the Lord will surely bestow with generous abundance.

I hope that the celebration of these days may be for you all a privileged occasion of formation and growth in the personal and community knowledge of Christ; may it be an interior stimulus to consecrate yourselves to the Church in the service of your brothers and sisters to build the civilization of love.

To Mary, the Virgin present in the Upper Room, the Mother of the Church (cf. *Acts* 1:14), I entrust the preparation and success of the next World Youth Days: may she share with us the secret of how to receive her Son into our lives so we may fulfil his will (cf. *John* 2:5).

May my heartfelt and paternal Blessing accompany you. (IX and X WYD 1994 and 1995)

And the Young People Reflect

Robert writes:

Each time I see young people with the Pope, I am
humbled to see the love and outpouring of faith
from all generations towards this gentle, elderly,
holy man. The kind of love and devotion one usually
finds among teens for sports players, rock stars or
movie stars is displayed for a Bishop, the Bishop of
Rome. The chants, whether they are "JP2" or "Jovani
Paulo," show the love and devotion his youth have
for him. This love and devotion that was earned by
his love and devotion to them. A love and devotion
that I share and have shared in.

. . . and Nicholas writes:

While you are listening to a homily or talk by the
Holy Father, it is difficult to really understand what
is being said. You hear his voice speaking in Italian
from the speakers, and then, slightly behind the
voice on the speakers you hear his voice on your
headphones, and then, finally, you hear the English
translation. Combined with incomparable enthusiasm and excitement, truly hearing the Holy Father's
message and reflecting upon it is nearly impossible.
After World Youth Day I read through his talks and
homilies and prayed about some of his words. I
looked over my journal and prayed about phrases
and events I forgot about in the hectic moments of
the trip.

. . . and Charles writes:

As a young person, I have to tap into my faith. I must be ready to answer the call of Jesus. Many great people who have shaped the history of the world in a positive way had a very tough life when they were young. They never lost sight of their goal in life. I must aim forward. I must accept myself the way I am and be ready to be taught and directed on the good to be done and evil to be avoided. We are most of the time inclined to what is fake and dull. This must change if we want to make this world a better place to live in.

. . . and Melissa writes:

The Holy Father continues to reach out to the youth and the whole world in His pursuit of holiness, to build his civilization of love. He was a mentor to me as a college student; I read his encyclicals, his books on philosophy, social teaching, and much more. Now as a young adult, I am in the midst of reading his biography. His life has been a distinct testimony to the beauty of God's grace when a single soul hands over their freedom to God's will so completely. Thank You, sweet Holy Father, for saying "Yes" to the Lord, not just yesterday, but every day. The world is indebted to your dedication and immensely blessed by your gift.

Paris, France
(19—24 August 1997)

Theme: "Teacher, where are you staying? Come and see" (*John* 1:38–39).

And so the Pope says:

Dear Young People!

I come to you with joy to continue the dialogue, already long, whose fabric we are weaving together on the occasion of the World Youth Day. In communion with the whole people of God on the journey towards the Great Jubilee of the Year 2000, I want to invite you this year to fix your eyes on Jesus, Teacher and Lord of life, with the help of the words recalled in John's Gospel: "Teacher, where are you staying? Come and see" (cf. 1:38–39).

In all the local Churches, during the coming months, you will be meeting together to reflect, with your Pastors, on these words of the Gospel. Then, in August 1997, together with many of you, we will have the experience of the XII World Youth Day, celebrated at international level in Paris, at the heart of the continent of Europe. In that metropolis, for centuries a crossroads for peoples, for art and culture, the young people of France are already preparing, enthusiastically, to welcome their young contemporaries from every corner of the planet.

Following the Holy Year Cross, the people of the younger generations who believe in Christ will, once again, become a living icon of the Church in her pilgrimage along the roads of the world. Meeting in prayer and reflection, in the dialogue that unites beyond all difference of language and race, in the sharing of ideals, problems and hopes, these young people will experience living the reality promised by Jesus: "Where two or three are gathered in my name, there am I in the midst of them" (*Matthew* 18:20).

Youth of the whole world, it is along the paths of daily life that you can meet the Lord! Do you remember how the disciples, hurrying to the banks of the Jordan to listen to the last of the great prophets, John the Baptist, saw Jesus of Nazareth pointed out to them as the Messiah, the Lamb of God? Out of curiosity they decided to follow Him at a distance. They were shy almost and embarrassed, until, turning round, He asked them: "What do you seek?" So began the dialogue that would give rise to the adventure of John, Andrew, Simon "Peter" and the other apostles (cf. *John* 1:29–51).

In this concrete and surprising encounter, described in a few, essential words, we find the origin of every journey in faith. It is Jesus who takes the initiative. When we have to do with Him, the question is always turned upside down: from questioners, we become questioned; "searchers", we discover that we are "sought"; He, indeed, has always loved us first (cf. 1 *John* 4:10). This is the fundamental dimension of the encounter: we are not dealing with something, but with Someone, with the "Living One". Christians are not the disciples of a system of philosophy: they are men and women who, in faith, have experienced the encounter with Christ (cf. 1 *John* 1:1–4).

When my thoughts go back to your words, spoken during the unforgettable encounters I have had the joy of experiencing with you on my apostolic journeys to every part of the world, I seem to read in them, with vital urgency, the very question of the disciples: "Teacher, where are you staying?" See that you are able to listen again, in the silence of prayer, to Jesus' answer: "Come and see".

Dear young people, like the first disciples, follow Jesus! Do not be afraid to draw near to Him, to cross the threshold of his dwelling, to speak with

Him, face to face, as you talk with a friend (cf. *Exodus* 33:11). Do not be afraid of the "new life" He is offering. He Himself makes it possible for you to receive that life and practise it, with the help of his grace and the gift of his Spirit.

It is true: Jesus is a demanding friend. He points to lofty goals; he asks us to go out of ourselves in order to meet Him, entrusting to Him our whole life: "Whoever loses his life for my sake and that of the Gospel will save it" (*Mark* 8:35). The proposal may seem difficult, and, in some cases, frightening. But— I ask you—is it better to be resigned to a life without ideals, to a world made in our image and likeness, or rather, generously to seek truth, goodness, justice, working for a world that reflects the beauty of God, even at the cost of facing the trials it may involve?

Break down the barriers of superficiality and fear! Recognizing that you are "new" men and women, regenerated by the grace of Baptism, talk with Jesus in prayer and while listening to the Word; experience the joy of reconciliation in the sacrament of Penance; receive the Body and Blood of Christ in the Eucharist; welcome and serve Him in your brothers and sisters. You will discover the truth about yourselves and your inner unity, and you will find a "Thou" who gives the cure for anxieties, for nightmares and for the unbridled subjectivism that leaves you no peace.

"Come and see". You will meet Jesus where men and women are suffering and hoping: in the little villages, scattered across the continents and seemingly on the fringe of history, as Nazareth was when God sent his Angel to Mary; in the huge metropolises, where millions of human beings live often as strangers. In reality, every human being is a "fellow citizen" of Christ.

Jesus is living next to you, in the brothers and sisters with whom you share your daily existence. His visage is that of the poorest, of the marginalized who, not infrequently, are victims of an unjust model of development, in which profit is given first place and the human being is made a means rather than an end. Jesus' dwelling is wherever a human person is suffering because rights are denied, hopes betrayed, anxieties ignored. There, in the midst of humankind, is the dwelling of Christ, who asks you to dry every tear in his name, and to remind whoever feels lonely that no one whose hope is placed in Him is ever alone (cf. *Matthew* 25:31–46).

Jesus dwells among those who call on Him without having known Him; among those who, after beginning to know Him, have lost Him through no fault of their own; among those who seek Him in sincerity of heart, while coming from different cultural and religious contexts (cf. *Lumen Gentium*, number 16). As disciples and friends of Jesus, become agents of dialogue and collaboration with those who believe in a God who rules the universe with infinite love; be ambassadors of the Messiah you have found and known in his "dwelling", the Church, so that many more young people of your age may be able to follow in his footsteps; their way lighted by your fraternal charity and by the joy in your eyes that have contemplated Christ.

Jesus dwells among the men and women "honoured with the name of Christian" (cf. *Lumen Gentium*, number 15). All are able to meet Him in the Scriptures, in prayer and in service of their neighbours. On the eve of the third millennium, it is becoming every day a more urgent duty to repair the scandal of the division among Christians, strengthening unity through dialogue, prayer in common and witness. It is not a matter of ignoring differences and problems in the detachment of a lukewarm relativism; that would be like covering the wound without healing it, with the risk of interrupting the journey before reaching the goal of full communion. On the contrary, it is a matter of working—under the guidance of the Holy Spirit—with a view to effective reconciliation, trusting in the efficacy of Jesus' prayer on the eve of his passion: "Father, that they may be one even as we are one" (cf. *John* 17:22). The more you cling to Jesus the more capable you will become of being close to one another; and insofar as you make concrete gestures of reconciliation you will enter into the intimacy of his love.

Jesus dwells especially in your parishes, in the communities in which you live, in the associations and ecclesial movements to which you belong, as well as in many contemporary forms of grouping and apostolate at the service of the new evangelization. This rich variety of charisms is a benefit for the whole Church, and an encouragement for every believer to place his or her capacities at the service of the one Lord, fount of salvation for all humankind.

Jesus is "the Word of the Father" (cf. *John* 1:1), gift to humankind, to reveal the face of God, and to give a meaning and goal to their uncertain steps. God who "spoke of old to our fathers by the prophets in many and various ways, has spoken to us by a Son, whom he appointed the heir of all things, through whom also he created the world" (*Hebrews* 1:1–2). His word is not an imposition, unhinging the doors of conscience; it is a persuasive voice, a free gift that, if it is to have a saving effect in each one's concrete existence, calls for an attitude of readiness and responsibility, a pure heart and a free mind.

In your groups, dear young people, multiply the occasions for hearing and studying the word of the Lord, especially through the *lectio divina*. You will discover the secrets of the Heart of God and will derive profit for discerning situations and transforming reality. Guided by Holy Scripture, you will be able to recognize the Lord's presence in your daily life; and even the "desert" can then become a "garden", where it is possible for the creature to talk familiarly with the Creator: "When I am reading divine Scripture, God walks again in the earthly Paradise" (Saint Ambrose, *Epistle* 49,3).

Jesus lives among us in the Eucharist, the supreme fulfilment of his real presence, a presence that is contemporary with the history of humankind. Amidst the uncertainties and distractions of daily life, imitate the disciples on their way to Emmaus; like them, say to the Risen One, revealed in the act of breaking the bread: "Stay with us, for it is toward evening and the day is now far spent" (*Luke* 24:29). Call out to Jesus to remain with you always along the many roads to Emmaus of our time. May He be your strength, your point of reference, your enduring hope. May the Eucharistic Bread, dear young people, never be lacking on the tables of your existence. And may you draw from this Bread the strength to bear witness to the faith!

Around the Eucharistic table the harmonious unity of the Church is realized and made manifest; the mystery of missionary communion, in which all feel that they are children, sisters and brothers, without any exclusion or difference from race, language, age, social situation or culture. Dear young people, make your generous and responsible contribution to the constant building up of the Church as a family, a place of dialogue and mutual acceptance, a space of peace, mercy and pardon.

Enlightened by the Word and strengthened by the Bread of the Eucharist, dear young people, you are called to be credible witnesses to the Gospel of Christ, who makes all things new.

But how are you to be recognized as true disciples of Christ? By the fact that you have "love for one another" (*John* 13:35) after the example of his love: a love that is freely given, infinitely patient and denied to no one (cf. *1 Corinthians* 13:4–7). Fidelity to the new commandment will be the guarantee that you are consistent with respect to what you are proclaiming.

In this world you are called to live fraternally, not as a utopia but as a real possibility; in this society you are called, as true missionaries of Christ, to build the civilization of love.

On 30 September 1997 will occur the centenary of the death of Saint Thérèse of Lisieux. Hers is a figure that, in her own country, cannot fail to draw the attention of a great many young pilgrims; Thérèse, precisely, is a young Saint, and her message today is simple and suggestive, brimming over with amazement and gratitude: God is Love; every person is loved by God, who expects to be welcomed and loved by each one. This is a message, young people of today, that you are called to receive and to shout aloud to those of your own age: "Man is loved by God! This very simple yet profound proclamation is owed to humanity by the Church" (cf. *Christifideles Laici,* number 34).

From the youth of Theresa of the Child Jesus spring forth her enthusiasm for the Lord, the intensity of her love, the realistic daring of her great projects. The charm of her holiness is confirmation that God grants in abundance, even to the young, the treasures of his wisdom.

Walk with her the humble and simple way of Christian maturity, at the school of the Gospel. Stay with her in the "heart" of the Church, living radically the option for Christ.

Dear young people, in the house where Jesus dwells meet the most sweet presence of the Mother. It is in Mary's womb that the Word was made flesh. Accepting the role assigned to her in the plan of salvation, the Virgin became a model for every disciple of Christ.

I entrust to Her the preparation and the celebration of the XII World Youth Day, together with the hopes and expectations of the young people who, with Her, are repeating in every corner of the planet: "Behold, I am the handmaid of the Lord; let it be done to me according to your word" (cf. *Luke* 1:38); and who are going to meet Jesus, to stay with Him, ready then to proclaim to their contemporaries, as did the Apostles: "We have found the Messiah!" (*John* 1:41).

With this message I cordially greet each one of you and, accompanying you with my prayer, I bless you. (XII WYD 1997)

And the Young People Reflect

Melissa writes:

World Youth Day 1997, in Paris, France, was one of the contributing factors of why I live the life I live today and every day. Some people may think this is a bit of a stretch in declaring that event as so important, but in my life, it was another wonderful example of love from the Lord. It was a time of deeper learning about Christ, His people, His Church and the bigger world out there. Coming from a family that cherished life and loved me so well, the seeds of obedience, commitment and genuine love were already being fostered. I had a strong desire to be someone for Jesus, to follow His Way of life and continue to learn about Him. As an active member of my parish youth ministry program, the idea of traveling to Paris, France, to see a man I truly honored and then to experience the cultures of the world on display within one setting seemed like a once in a lifetime opportunity, a wonderful adventure. I was seventeen and eager to find out what God had in store for my little life.

Though young and some may think, naively passionate, we energized the Holy Father and he excited us. It was a relationship of reciprocal love and admiration. This man was a real testament to the message he proclaimed, and with his past and current actions and experiences as his proof of knowledge, wisdom, and understanding of the human heart, we were ready to follow him to the ends of the earth. In this way, I can understand the desire of the apostles to follow Christ. From the gift of the Holy Father's love and a true encounter with Jesus in my own heart, I too wanted to follow Christ and see where he dwelt.

. . . and Charles writes:

I look at our Pope as a good example of how young people in Africa can rise above the sufferings we are undergoing and make it to the top, achieve our goals. The Pope's background, when he was young, is not pleasing at all. He never grew up in a King's court or a palace. He struggled as a young person. Each day was a mountain to be climbed, and with courage each step got easier. He made it!

. . . and Robert writes:

The dark night had fallen and the formerly scorching heat had subsided to a cold breeze. Most of the Boston contingent had left the field around midnight. To my knowledge at that moment, we were the only ones from the Archdiocese left in the field. Three members of our group were already in the hospital tents; we had lost touch with them hours before. I remember vividly how tired and hungry we all were. Rumors had been flying fast and furious after sunset that the food tents had run out of food and that the sanitation facilities were overwhelmed. This wasn't quite how I had pictured World Youth Day was going to be.

. . . and Andrei writes:

The Holy Father is not an entertainer, even if he is such a pleasant host, and the millions of voices cheering him a few minutes before would not divert him: like Saint John the Baptist, the Pope was aware he was not the Messiah, even if on that evening he had an audience by far larger than Christ had ever had in His life on earth. He was there to help the young people and, through them, the youth of the world, in their search, to give a name to their quest for happiness, joy, truth, love and peace: Jesus Christ!

Rome, Italy
(15–20 August 2000)

Theme: "The Word became flesh and dwelt among us"
(*John* 1:14).

And so the Pope says:

My dear young people

Fifteen years ago, at the close of the Holy Year of the Redemption, I entrusted to you a great wooden Cross, asking you to carry it across the world as a sign of the love which the Lord Jesus has for mankind and to proclaim to everyone that only in Christ who died and is risen is there salvation and redemption. Since that day, carried by generous hands and hearts, the Cross has made a long, uninterrupted pilgrimage across the continents, to demonstrate that the Cross walks with young people and young people walk with the Cross.

Around the "Holy Year Cross", World Youth Days were born and developed as meaningful "moments of rest" along your journey as young Christians; a constant, pressing invitation to build life on the rock that is Christ. How can we fail to bless the Lord for the countless fruits born in the hearts of individuals and in the whole Church thanks to the World Youth Days, which in this last part of the century have marked the journey of young believers towards the new millennium?

After spanning the continents, that Cross now returns to Rome bringing with it the prayers and commitment of millions of young people who have recognized it as a simple and sacred sign of God's love for humanity. Because Rome, as you know, will host World Youth Day of the Year 2000, in the heart of the Great Jubilee.

Dear young people, I invite you therefore to undertake with joy the pilgrimage to Rome for this important ecclesial appointment, which will rightly be the "Youth Jubilee". Prepare to enter the Holy Door, knowing that to pass through it is to strengthen faith in Him in order to live the new life which he has given to us (cf. *Incarnationis Mysterium*, paragraph 8).

I chose as the theme for your 15th World Day the lapidary phrase with which Saint John the Apostle describes the profound mystery of God made man: "The Word became flesh, and dwelt among us" (*John* 1:14). What distinguishes the Christian faith from all other religions, is the certainty that the man Jesus of Nazareth is the Son of God, the Word made flesh, the second person of the Trinity who came into the world.

God, the invisible one is alive and present in the person of Jesus, Son of Mary, the Theotokos, Mother of God. Jesus of Nazareth is God with us, Emmanuel: he who knows Him knows God, he who sees Him sees God, he who follows Him follows God, he who unites himself with Him is united with God (cf. *John* 12:44–50). In Jesus, born in Bethlehem, God embraces the human condition, making himself accessible, establishing a covenant with mankind.

On the eve of the new millennium, I make again to you my pressing appeal to open wide the doors to Christ who "to those who received him, gave power to become children of God" (*John* 1:12). To receive Jesus Christ means to accept from the Father the command to live, loving Him and our brothers and sisters, showing solidarity to everyone, without distinction; it means believing that in the history of humanity even though it is marked by evil and suffering, the final word belongs to life and to love, because God came to dwell among us, so we may dwell in Him.

By his incarnation Christ became poor to enrich us with his poverty, and he gave us redemption, which is the fruit above all of the blood he shed on the Cross (cf. *Catechism of the Catholic Church*, number 517). On Calvary, "ours were the sufferings he bore . . . he was pierced through for our faults" (*Isaiah* 53: 4–5). The supreme sacrifice of his life, freely given for our salvation, is the proof of God's infinite love for us. Saint John the Apostle writes: "God loved the world so much that he gave his only Son so that everyone that believes in him may not be lost but may have eternal life" (*John* 3:16).

Jesus went towards his death. He did not draw back from any of the consequences of his being "with us", Emmanuel. He took our place, ransoming us on the Cross from evil and sin (cf. *Evangelium Vitae*, number 50). Just as the Roman Centurion, seeing the manner in which Jesus died, understood that he was the Son of God (cf. *Mark* 15:39) so we too, seeing and contemplating the Crucified Lord, understand who God really is, as he reveals in Jesus the depth of his love for mankind (cf. *Redemptor Hominis*, number 9).

"Passion" means a passionate love, unconditioned self-giving: Christ's passion is the summit of an entire life "given" to his brothers and sisters to reveal the heart of the Father. The Cross, which seems to rise up from the earth, in actual fact reaches down from heaven, enfolding the universe in a divine embrace. The Cross reveals itself to be "the centre, meaning and goal of all history and of every human life" (*Evangelium Vitae*, number 50).

Behind the death of Jesus there is a plan of love, which the faith of the Church calls the "mystery of the redemption": the whole of humanity is redeemed, that is, set free from the slavery of sin and led into the kingdom of God. Christ is Lord of heaven and earth. Whoever listens to his word and believes in the Father, who sent him, has eternal life (cf. *John* 5:25). He is the "Lamb of God who takes away the sins of the world" (*John* 1:29–36), the high priest who, having suffered like us, is able to share our infirmity (cf. *Hebrews* 4:14) and "made perfect" through the painful experience of the Cross, becomes "for all who obey him, the source of eternal salvation" (*Hebrews* 5:9).

Dear young people, faced with these great mysteries, learn to lift your hearts in an attitude of contemplation. Stop and look with wonder at the infant Mary brought into the world, wrapped in swaddling clothes and laid in a manger: the infant is God himself who has come among us. Look at Jesus of Nazareth, received by some and scorned by others, despised and rejected: He is the Saviour of all. Adore Christ, our Redeemer, who ransoms us and frees us from sin and death: He is the living God, the source of Life.

Contemplate and reflect! God created us to share in his very own life; he calls us to be his children, living members of the mystical Body of Christ, luminous temple of the Spirit of Love. He calls us to be his: he wants us all to be saints. Dear young people, may it be your holy ambition to be holy, as He is holy.

You will ask me: but is it possible today to be saints? If we had to rely only on human strength, the undertaking would be truly impossible. You are well aware, in fact, of your successes and your failures; you are aware of the heavy burdens weighing on man, the many dangers which threaten him and the consequences caused by his sins. At times we may be gripped by discouragement and even come to think that it is impossible to change anything either in the world or in ourselves.

Although the journey is difficult, we can do everything in the One who is our Redeemer. Turn then to no one, except Jesus. Do not look elsewhere for that which only He can give you, because "of all the names in the world given to men this is the only one by which we can be saved" (*Acts* 4:12). With Christ, saintliness—the divine plan for every baptized person—becomes possible. Rely on Him; believe in the invincible power of the Gospel and place faith as the foundation of your hope. Jesus walks with you, he renews your heart and strengthens you with the vigour of his Spirit.

Young people of every continent, do not be afraid to be the saints of the new millennium! Be contemplative, love prayer; be coherent with your faith and generous in the service of your brothers and sisters, be active members of the Church and builders of peace. To succeed in this demanding project of life, continue to listen to His Word, draw strength from the Sacraments, especially the Eucharist and Penance. The Lord wants you to be intrepid apostles of his Gospel and builders of a new humanity. In fact, how could you say you believe in God made man without taking a firm position against all that destroys the human person and the family? If you believe that Christ has revealed the Father's love for every person, you cannot fail to strive to contribute to the building of a new world, founded on the power of love and forgiveness, on the struggle against injustice and all physical, moral and spiritual distress, on the orientation of politics, economy, culture and technology to the service of man and his integral development.

I sincerely wish that the Jubilee, now at the door, may be an opportune time for courageous spiritual renewal and an exceptional celebration of God's love for humanity. From the whole Church may there rise up "a hymn of praise and thanksgiving to the Father, who in his incomparable love granted us in Christ to be 'fellow citizens with the saints and members of the household of God'" (*Incarnationis Mysterium*, paragraph 6). May we draw comfort from the certainty expressed by Saint Paul the Apostle: If God did not spare his only Son but gave him for us, how can he fail to give us everything with him? Who can separate us from the love of Christ? In every event of life, including death, we can be more than winners, by virtue of the One who loved us to the Cross (cf. *Romans* 8:31–37).

The mystery of the Incarnation of the Son of God and that of the Redemption he worked for all men, constitute the central message of our faith. The Church proclaims this down through the centuries . . . and she entrusts it to her children as a precious treasure to be safeguarded and shared.

You too, dear young people, are the receivers and the trustees of this heritage. We will proclaim it together on the occasion of the next World Youth Day, in which I hope very many of you will take part. Rome is a "city-shrine" where the memory of the Apostles Peter and Paul and other martyrs remind pilgrims of the vocation of every baptized person. Before the world, in August next year, we will repeat the profession of faith made by Saint Peter the Apostle: "Lord to whom shall we go? You have the words of eternal life" (*John* 6:68) because "you are the Christ the Son of the Living God!" (*Matthew* 16:16).

The Incarnation of the Word and the Redemption of mankind are closely linked with the Annunciation when God revealed to Mary his plan and found in her, a young person like yourselves, a heart totally open to the action of his love. For centuries Christian devotion has recalled every day, with the recitation of the *Angelus Domini,* God's entrance into the history of man. May this prayer become your daily meditated prayer.

Mary is the dawn which precedes the rising of the Sun of justice, Christ our Redeemer. With her "yes" at the Annunciation, as she opened herself completely to Father's plan, she welcomed and made possible the incarnation of the Son. The first disciple, with her discreet presence she accompanied Jesus all the way to Calvary and sustained the hope of the Apostles as they waited for the Resurrection and Pentecost. In the life of the Church she continues to be mystically the one who precedes the Lord's coming.

To Mary, who fulfills without interruption her ministry as Mother of the Church and of each Christian, I entrust with confidence the preparation of the 15th World Youth Day. May Most Holy Mary teach you, dear young people, how to discern the will of the heavenly Father in your life. May she obtain for you the strength and the wisdom to speak to God and to speak about God. Through her example may she encourage you to be in the new millennium announcers of hope, love and peace.

Looking forward to meeting many of you in Rome next year, "I commend you to God, and to the word of his grace that has power to build you up and to give you your inheritance among all the sanctified" (*Acts* 20:32), while, gladly and with great affection, I bless all of you, with your families and your loved ones. (XV WYD 2000)

And the Young People Reflect

Andrei writes:

My fellow volunteers came from all over Romania, youth of the Latin and Byzantine rites of the Catholic Church, boys and girls between twenty and thirty years old. During the long way by bus, when we were not sleeping, we would sing, pray together and try to get to know each other, so that when we got to Rome, if we were not yet a team, we had become friends.

It was August and it was very hot. Liceo Augusto hosted up to 200 volunteers, coming from Italy, France and Romania. We slept with the windows open, but it did not make much difference. Early in the morning, around 6 a.m., a sharp sound wakes us up: a bugle. One of the French volunteers, who had a bugle, had the great idea to wake all the volunteers lodging in Augusto, like in an army base. We were not exactly happy for the abrupt manner in which our day began, but as we got used to it, we got to like it and even missed it when we left.

Our first great mission was to go to a high school outside Rome and to help prepare it for the pilgrims who would be lodged there. We were supposed to be there early in the morning because it was a big high school. We had to clean the gym, to take the desks from the classes and store them in a different place, dust the rooms and mop them. It wasn't very difficult and we enjoyed working together. We all had friends or relatives who would be coming as pilgrims, so it was like preparing for their arrival.

Another day we were allotted to the service of the Basilica San Paolo fuori le mura, one of the four patriarchal basilicas of Rome. Before the arrival of the pilgrims, we were given a tour of the basilica by a professional guide and we were explained our duties. We were supposed to see that the pilgrims would be dressed modestly (and it was not always easy, for it was in the middle of August!), that they would observe silence and that they would use the right ways of access. Some of us were there to help people on the way to the toilets or to give directions. It was interesting to look at the different types of pilgrims, some very devout, kneeling on the threshold of the Holy Door and praying the indulgence prayers, some ignoring the significance of the Basilica for the Jubilee, more interested in the artistic beauty of the church.

One afternoon, some of my fellow volunteers from Sicily wanted to visit the church where the relics of Saint Thérèse of Lisieux were exposed during the World Youth Days. It was a small church, hidden among other buildings, Santa Maria in Capranica, very fitting for the saint of *the little way*. There were many pilgrims in line to venerate the relics of the Little Flower. As I got closer, I met my brother, who had come as a pilgrim. It was the first time we would meet since we had arrived, and we were both grateful to the Little Flower for this double grace, of getting to pray before her bier and of meeting, something that we didn't even dream of with all those pilgrims.

. . . and Gail writes:

Though the WYD was long and tiring, it made me realize what a truly wonderful place we live in. Being in the presence of such a great and noble man was a once-in-a-lifetime experience. I will always remember the chants from the crowds of "JPII, we love you!!!"

Typically one of the greatest highlights for most people attending World Youth Day is the pilgrimage to the overnight Vigil and the papal Mass. The experience of World Youth Day took place by participating in the larger events such as the Vigil and papal Mass, but also profoundly in the smaller happenings of people such as after the evening prayer service. Of the ceremony, the most memorable part was holding one of two million candles, symbolizing our light in the darkness. After the service, the Holy Father joked it was past his bedtime, fireworks lit up the sky and a nearby Sister quite fittingly commented, "All this and heaven."

We then were free to walk around and meet new people. A few friends and I casually joined in with many others who were doing a cultural dance or praying. We would often trade things from our hometowns, like pins or pencils. One best trade was a T-shirt from my home parish for an Italian flag with the words "And the Phenomenon . . . We have Wojtyla!" As I expected there were numerous communication barriers, but each time there was always an extended welcome.

My pilgrimage to World Youth Day 2000 led me to travel to World Youth Day 2002 where I was blessed to live with my people throughout the world. One of my most memorable experiences came while serving lunch to some people in my group. I asked everyone their name and where they were from. One man responded, "My name is Niaz. I'm from Iraq." I responded, saying, "Oh . . . I'm Nick and from the United States." After a moment of silence, Niaz asserted, "It is unfortunate we are enemies on the political level, but on a deeper level we are brothers in Christ."

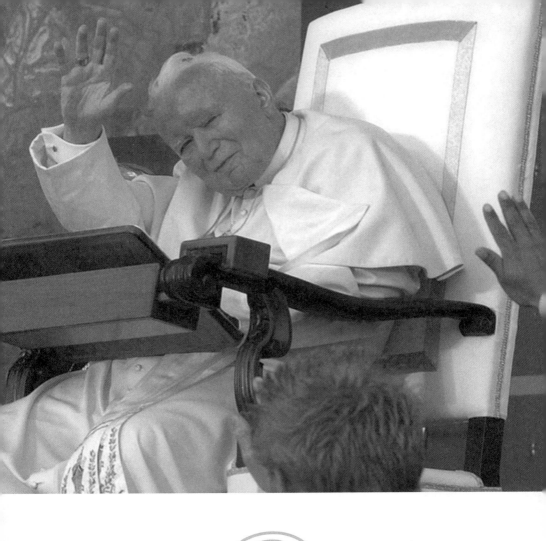

Toronto, Canada
(23–28 July 2002)

Theme: "You are the salt of the earth . . . you are the light of the world" (*Matthew* 5:13,14).

And so the Pope says:

Dear Young People!
    I have vivid memories of the wonderful moments we shared in Rome during the Jubilee of the Year 2000, when you came on pilgrimage to the Tombs of the Apostles Peter and Paul. In long silent lines you passed through the Holy Door and prepared to receive the Sacrament of Reconciliation; then the Evening Vigil and Morning Mass at Tor Vergata were moments of intense spirituality and a deep experience of the Church; with renewed faith, you went home to undertake the mission I entrusted to you: to become, at the dawn of the new millennium, fearless witnesses to the Gospel.
    By now World Youth Day has become an important part of your life and of the life of the Church. I invite you therefore to get ready for the seventeenth celebration of this great international event, to be held in Toronto, Canada, in the summer of next year. It will be another chance to meet Christ, to bear witness to his presence in today's society, and to become builders of the "civilization of love and truth".
    "You are the salt of the earth . . . You are the light of the world" (*Matthew* 5:13–14): this is the theme I have chosen for the next World Youth Day. The images of salt and light used by Jesus are rich in meaning and complement each other. In ancient times, salt and light were seen as essential elements of life.
    "You are the salt of the earth . . ." One of the main functions of salt is to season food, to give it

taste and flavour. This image reminds us that, through Baptism, our whole being has been profoundly changed, because it has been "seasoned" with the new life which comes from Christ (cf. *Romans* 6:4). The salt which keeps our Christian identity intact even in a very secularized world is the grace of Baptism.

Through Baptism we are re-born. We begin to live in Christ and become capable of responding to his call to "offer [our] bodies as a living sacrifice, holy and acceptable to God" (*Romans* 12:1). Writing to the Christians of Rome, Saint Paul urges them to show clearly that their way of living and thinking was different from that of their contemporaries: "Do not be conformed to this world, but be transformed by the renewal of your mind, that you may discern what is the will of God, what is good and pleasing and perfect" (*Romans* 12:2).

Discover your Christian roots, learn about the Church's history, deepen your knowledge of the spiritual heritage which has been passed on to you, follow in the footsteps of the witnesses and teachers who have gone before you! Only by staying faithful to God's commandments, to the Covenant which Christ sealed with his blood poured out on the Cross, will you be the apostles and witnesses of the new millennium.

It is the nature of human beings, and especially youth, to seek the Absolute, the meaning and fullness of life. Dear young people, do not be content with anything less than the highest ideals! Do not let yourselves be dispirited by those who are disillusioned with life and have grown deaf to the deepest and most authentic desires of their heart. You are right to be disappointed with hollow entertainment and passing fads, and with aiming at too little in life. If you have an ardent desire for the Lord you will steer clear of the mediocrity and conformism so widespread in our society.

"You are the light of the world . . ." For those who first heard Jesus, as for us, the symbol of light evokes the desire for truth and the thirst for the fullness of knowledge which are imprinted deep within every human being.

When the light fades or vanishes altogether, we no longer see things as they really are. In the heart of the night we can feel frightened and insecure, and we impatiently await the coming of the light of dawn. Dear young people, it is up to you to be the watchmen of the morning (cf. *Isaiah* 21:11–12) who announce the coming of the sun who is the Risen Christ!

The light which Jesus speaks of in the Gospel is the light of faith, God's free gift, which enlightens the heart and clarifies the mind. "It is the God who said, 'Let light shine out of darkness', who has shone in our hearts to give the light of the knowledge of the glory of God on the face of Christ" (*2 Corinthians* 4:6). That is why the words of Jesus explaining his identity and his mission are so important: "I am the light of the world; whoever follows me will not walk in darkness, but will have the light of life" (*John* 8:12).

Our personal encounter with Christ bathes life in new light, sets us on the right path, and sends us out to be his witnesses. This new way of looking at the world and at people, which comes to us from him, leads us more deeply into the mystery of faith, which is not just a collection of theoretical assertions to be accepted and approved by the mind, but an experience to be had, a truth to be lived, the salt and light of all reality (cf. *Veritatis Splendor*, number 88).

In this secularized age, when many of our contemporaries think and act as if God did not exist or are attracted to irrational forms of religion, it is you, dear young people, who must show that faith is a personal decision which involves your whole life. Let the Gospel be the measure and guide of life's decisions and plans! Then you will be missionaries in all that you do and say, and wherever you work and live you will be signs of God's love, credible witnesses to the loving presence of Jesus Christ. Never forget: "No one lights a lamp and then puts it under a bushel" (*Matthew* 5:15)!

Just as salt gives flavour to food and light illumines the darkness, so too holiness gives full meaning to life and makes it reflect God's glory. How many saints, especially young saints, can we count in the Church's history! In their love for God their heroic virtues shone before the world, and so they became models of life which the Church has held up for imitation by all. Let us remember only a few of them: Agnes of Rome, Andrew of Phú Yên, Pedro Calungsod, Josephine Bakhita, Thérèse of Lisieux, Pier Giorgio Frassati, Marcel Callo, Francisco Castelló Aleu or again Kateri Tekakwitha, the young Iroquois called "the Lily of the Mohawks". Through the intercession of this great host of witnesses, may God make you too, dear young people, the saints of the third millennium!

Dear friends, it is time to get ready for the Seventeenth World Youth Day. I invite you to read and study the Apostolic Letter *Novo Millennio Ineunte*, which I wrote at the beginning of the year to accompany all Christians on this new stage of the life of the Church and humanity: "A new century, a new millennium are opening in the light of Christ. But not everyone can see this light. Ours is the wonderful and demanding task of becoming its 'reflection'" (number 54).

Yes, now is the time for mission! In your Dioceses and parishes, in your movements, associations and communities, Christ is calling you. The Church welcomes you and wishes to be your home and your school of communion and prayer. Study the Word of God and let it enlighten your minds and hearts. Draw strength from the sacramental grace of Reconciliation and the Eucharist. Visit the Lord in that "heart to heart" contact that is Eucharistic Adoration. Day after day, you will receive new energy to help you to bring comfort to the suffering and peace to the world. Many people are wounded by life: they are excluded from economic progress, and are without a home, a family, a job; there are people who are lost in a world of false illusions, or have abandoned all hope. By contemplating the light radiant on the face of the Risen Christ, you will learn to live as "children of the light and children of the day" (*1 Thessalonians* 5:5), and in this way you will show that "the fruit of light is found in all that is good and right and true" (*Ephesians* 5:9).

Dear young friends, Toronto is waiting for all of you who can make it! In the heart of a multi-cultural and multi-faith city, we shall speak of Christ as the one Saviour and proclaim the universal salvation of which the Church is the sacrament. In response to the pressing invitation of the Lord who ardently desires "that all may be one" (*John* 17:11), we shall pray for full communion among Christians in truth and charity.

Come, and make the great avenues of Toronto resound with the joyful tidings that Christ loves every person and brings to fulfilment every trace of goodness, beauty and truth found in the city of man. Come, and tell the world of the happiness you have found in meeting Jesus Christ, of your desire to know him better, of how you are committed to proclaiming the Gospel of salvation to the ends of the earth!

The young people of Canada, together with their Bishops and the civil authorities, are already preparing to welcome you with great warmth and hospitality. For this I thank them all from my heart. May this first World Youth Day of the new millennium bring to everyone a message of faith, hope and love!

My blessing goes with you. And to Mary Mother of the Church I entrust each one of you, your vocation and your mission. (XVII WYD 2002)

And the Young People Reflect

Anthony writes:

I was very excited the morning of my visit with the Pope. What an unbelievable experience. When I got into the van to go to Toronto, I asked my mom to bring my rosary ring. All the way, from Hamilton to Young Street in Toronto, I prayed with the ring. When I received my invitation and saw that I was a guest of the prime minister, I was shocked. When I got to the airport hangar, my mom and I talked to the prime minister's wife. It was an honour and a privilege to take a picture with the prime minister and his wife. And seeing the Holy Father in person, not only on TV or in the newspaper, but in person— you cannot put a price on that! When I met the pontiff face to face and I spoke those words to him, "Blessed be Jesus and Mary," in my (Croatian) language—it was amazing. I could not help but burst into tears. All my life I have been a very religious person. At the age of nine I suffered a severe stroke. The doctors told my mom that I was going to die, then that I would never walk again. They also said that I would be a "vegetable" for the rest of my life. I have proved them all wrong. I can walk on my own in the water with my new walker. With my physical disability it's hard sometimes but through prayer and the grace of God, it has gotten easier. I know my disability is hard on my family and it's hard for me too.

. . . and Robert writes:

I remember exclaiming how amazing it was to meet youth from around the world. Everywhere you went you heard different languages and saw hundreds of flags flying from countries that in some cases we had never heard of.

. . . and Gail writes:

These young people gave him a reception that was very much like that of a rock star; they wanted him to keep playing another encore. I still have goose bumps. I have never before experienced the thrill of seeing 200,000 young people so in love with their faith. World Youth Day helped me see past the Church scandals and made me realize that as a Church we will survive and flourish in the new millennium. These young people, the future leaders, will make it happen. They have made Pope John Paul II into a living icon, a vibrant example of their faith.

. . . and Nicholas writes:

It is amazing the images you will not forget: the Franciscan Friar praying on his knees, the girl so moved in prayer that she would not look up despite all the commotion around her, the last night when each country represented in a group sang their national anthem which totaled at least fifteen songs, the Spanish pilgrims dancing through the streets as we ate outside. At World Youth Day I found something that many people realize when they travel abroad: how similar the human race is. Despite our language, race and ethnicity differences, I knew the other youth and I shared a lot; we have the same questions, hopes, fears and aspirations.

Communication with others was often a struggle, yet amazingly this inability to converse put things into perspective. While we could not even say "hi" we had something so much deeper in common: our faith. As I wrote in my journal, "It's amazing how we can't even talk to each other but the more important thing we share—our faith. I've so much in common with people I never met before."

. . . and Melissa writes:

I also had a deep admiration for the Holy Father, John Paul II. Learning about his struggles in life, hearing his words of wisdom on TV when he had come to visit the United States, and seeing his genuine expressions of love to the poor and needy, I developed a profound respect for his mission and message. He was the only Pope I had known, and I was drawn to his nature from the very beginning.

. . . and Charles writes:

The words of our Pope shed some light in our lives as young people in Kenya, Africa. As young people we are the flowers whose fruits the whole world is waiting to see. The kind of young people we are will determine the kind of society we will have in the future.

. . . and Gottfried writes:

When we arrived in, I heard that only some people on the buses in our group could stay with families and I just thought to myself: "It will never be our bus, but to sleep in big halls, as we already did on our trip, is not at all a big problem!" But God amazed me once again and we stayed with a very loving family. They even spoke German and helped me to speak English.

. . . and Andrei writes:

The pavement stones of the square, heated by the sun during the whole day, were so hot that one could not sit on them. There was a gigantic water hose that would sprinkle the youth with water. Then the Holy Father came. Everyone cheered: "JP 2, we love you!"

Those who, like me, came from countries where the Church manifested its faithfulness to Christ by its bloody martyrdom, treasured the Pope's words particularly. Greek-Catholic bishops in Romania were promised to become Orthodox bishops and even metropolitans if only they abjured their fidelity to Peter and his successor. But, as one of them put it, their conscience was not for sale. As a result, all were sent to prison and five of them died there. They did follow the Lamb where He led, to the Cross, and did it joyously for the privilege of giving their lives, just as the first Christians, for Christ.

Journey of the World Youth Day Cross

The World Youth Day Cross

As this book began with the cross, so it ends with the Cross. In the second chapter of this book, you read about the presentation of a cross to the young people of Rome. How did this cross become known as the official World Youth Day Cross?

During the Holy Year of Redemption (1983–1984), Pope John Paul II believed that the symbol of our faith—a cross—should stand near the main altar in Saint Peter's Basilica. In accordance with the Pope's wishes, a cross was created and placed there.

At the end of the Holy Year, the Pope entrusted the cross to the youth of the San Lorenzo Youth Centre in Rome. The Pope told the young people to make that symbol of faith visible to the world, and so the young people began to carry the cross to celebrations where young people gathered and especially when they gathered together with the Holy Father. Before long, the cross became the Cross—the symbol of World Youth Days.

The World Youth Day Cross is one of the visible and tangible signs of the Church's faith in young Catholics, and of the love of the Pope for the youth of the world. Regardless of the year or the location, wherever the World Youth Day Cross is found, young people are also there. And whenever the young Church gathers for World Youth Day around the Cross, the Pope is there as well.

The experiences of World Youth Day continue to grow as the years pass, and the Cross continues to grow in meaning as well. This Cross, given to the young people of Italy so many years ago, has become the most powerful symbol of these international celebrations and gatherings of the world's youth. This symbol of faith is known as the Holy Year Cross, the Jubilee Cross, the WYD Cross, and the Pilgrim Cross. This Cross has traveled the world as a sign of hope for all. (See also "Pilgrimage of the Cross," on the Vatican Web site at *www.vatican.va.*)

On Palm Sunday, 2003, Pope John Paul II introduced a new element to the journey of the cross.

> Today I also entrust to the delegation from Germany the Icon of Mary. From now on it will accompany the World Youth Days, together with the Cross. Behold, your Mother! It will be a sign of Mary's motherly presence close to young people who are called, like the Apostle John, to welcome her into their lives. ("Angelus," XVIII WYD 2003)

The Cross continues its journey toward the next celebration of World Youth Day, touching lives and touching hearts with the power of its truth.

Chris writes:

> Several thousand people came out onto the streets of Glasgow in mid-February to welcome the World Youth Day Cross for the final leg of its Scottish pilgrimage. On Tuesday, 10 February, the cross was handed over by Motherwell Diocese to pupils of Saint Aidan's School, Carntyne. After a few problems trying to locate a large enough van—it almost ended up on the 4:29 train from Carfin to Glasgow Central—the 3.8-metre-tall cross was welcomed into Saint Andrew's Cathedral by a gathering of young people who had participated in recent World Youth Day pilgrimages.
>
> This was a solemn moment as the impressive cross was processed in slowly by a dozen young adults. Fr. Hugh McGinlay reminded us that in the week of Valentine's Day, the Cross represented "the greatest love letter" we will ever receive, the sign of the kind of love God has for all people. With that, we formally passed on John Paul II's invitation to the young people of our diocese to come to the next

World Youth Day in Cologne, Germany, in August 2005.

Many of us had seen the Cross from a distance at previous World Youth Day events, but to be so close to it was remarkably moving. Millions of young people have prayed around this Cross in every continent since the Pope first presented it in 1984.

Looking at its gnarled surface and scratched plaque reminded us of the spiritual "weight" it represents. We can speak quite glibly about carrying the cross in our lives, but the impact of the phrase hits home in a gut way when you are holding a life-sized replica.

Young people grasped the meaning of the Cross intuitively as they grasped the wood, holding it tenderly, reverently and with a sense of real dignity.

The stark nature of the Cross and its awesome significance came into even sharper focus on that bright crisp Wednesday morning as we gathered once more at Saint Andrew's Cathedral.

After Mass, some 60 people, including pupils and staff of Lourdes Secondary began the first leg of our marathon pilgrimage through Glasgow to Bearsden. In the precinct with the great cathedral of Saint Mungo as a backdrop, we held an ecumenical prayer service, acknowledging how members of the Church of Scotland have participated in recent World Youth Days. We committed ourselves as young people to an authentic ecumenical journey with our fellow Christians and to work towards eradicating all forms of religious intolerance in our city.

From the Cathedral we crossed to Saint Mungo's church, Townhead, passing the Royal Infirmary where the cross of illness is daily borne. Along with pupils from Saint Mungo's, Saint Kevin's and Saint Stephen's schools, we celebrated the parish morning Mass with the Passionist community. The Cross looked even bigger next to the primary pupils as they carried it into the sanctuary where it had last stood in 1985 on its first and only previous journey in Scotland.

The city-centre leg of the pilgrimage was easily the strangest. Our numbers had swelled to 80 as pupils from Saint Mungo's, Saint Roch's and All Saints secondaries joined in. Our two police cyclists had their work cut out for them as we briskly processed through the city.

People reacted in a variety of ways. There was simple annoyance as we cut across traffic and clogged the pavements. Others presumed we were a peace march or a political demo—despite the fact that we only carried the Cross, the Saltire and the Papal flag. Most folk smiled and waved.

You could see the nuisance factor disappear as people saw that we weren't just a street gang of troublesome youth—rather we were a street gang of troublesome youth carrying the Cross of Jesus Christ through the city as an act of witness to our faith.

As well as the sense of reverence, what struck me was the *ordinariness* of it all.

In the liturgy, we're accustomed to the notion that God takes ordinary things, bread and wine, and transforms them into the most extraordinary gift of his own flesh and blood. This kind of ordinary and yet extraordinary quality existed on our pilgrimage.

The pupils who carried the Cross were not particularly unusual, chosen or experienced. They were tall, small, skinny, round, loud, quiet, female and male—God's own little people. They were sometimes silent, sometimes raucous as they yelled warnings and instructions to one another about passing traffic or pedestrians. Despite the unusual circumstances, they understood exactly what we were doing. In an age when young people are presumed to be either hostile or indoctrinated to religious matters, our pilgrims were neither. They had opted into a pilgrimage because they wanted to tell people about the meaning of their lives and enjoy themselves with their peers.

Once we had crossed over the M8 flyover, we made our way up towards Saint Columba's parish, passing by Karol Path, named after John Paul II. Again we were welcomed by a nearly full church of young people, parents, parishioners and grandparents as well as several school chaplains and pupils from Saint Margaret Mary's and Our Lady's High.

Fr. David Trainer opened our prayer service drawing our attention to the boat-shaped inspiration of the church's design. This enabled the young pilgrims to realise that they were following Columba's own path of announcing the good news to the people of Scotland.

Then it was onwards up Maryhill Road to the parish of Immaculate Conception, where pupils and staff from John Paul Academy led the prayers of intercession with Fr. John Mulholland. Again the church was full, with pupils from Saint Gregory's and Saint Blaine's primaries joining in along with those from Saint Andrew's High, Clydebank. Older parishioners showed a great warmth and enthusiasm for our band of pilgrims, greeting them with applause as they arrived—only half an hour late!

This gave wonderful expression to the fact that we all belong to a whole church of people from cradle to grave, rather than being an isolated group tucked away in schools, youth clubs or out of the church altogether. Father Trainer reflected this when he said that the young people were ministering to him and his parish community.

As well as visiting churches, we passed shops, banks, houses, Paddy's Market, the concert hall, cinema, a fire station, hospital, museum, universities, office blocks, the building where asylum cases are processed, a Police Station, bus and train stations, and Partick Thistle football ground. All, in a sense, contemporary stations of the cross.

It must have been like this for Jesus in Jerusalem, making his way with the cross along the Via Dolorosa as daily life went on. You couldn't help but have a vivid street level sense of the bustle of Glasgow with all the people facing their daily "joys and hopes, grief and anguish" as the Second Vatican Council described it.

Although many folk noticed us, more didn't—a poignant reminder of the challenge we face in our attempts to speak of Jesus to today's world. We did not face the outright hostility or violence as Christ did, but being ignored or discounted as irrelevant is perhaps the new face of anti-Christian sentiment.

After some six hours walking and praying, we arrived at Scotus College where Cardinal O'Brien, Archbishop Conti and Bishops Mone, Murray, and Moran welcomed the pilgrimage on behalf of the Bishops' Conference of Scotland.

The Cardinal led a catechesis session, reflecting on his recent visit to Rwanda, where the shadow of the cross still hangs heavily ten years after an evil genocide ripped the country apart, claiming a million lives.

Just as the cross has been changed from an instrument of torture into a symbol of love, the Cardinal highlighted the efforts being made towards justice and reconciliation: "This is the Paschal mystery in action, when the power of God's love, through his people, can bring light and new life even in the most horrible human catastrophes."

Later, during the celebration of Mass, he encouraged and challenged the young people to recognise their own dignity as images of God and to take up the cross with dedication and hope in their day-to-day lives.

To round out a most memorable day in the company of the Cross, we returned in the evening to Saint Mungo's, Townhead, where Fr. Paul Francis Spencer and members of the parish youth group led a meditation on the Passion and Stations of the Cross in a beautiful candlelit vigil.

After such a hectic, limb-sapping but invigorating experience, the last day of our hosting the Cross was more reflective.

Archbishop Conti celebrated Mass at Our Lady of Consolation—recently set aside as a resource for diocesan youth ministry. He shared the story of his own Episcopal pectoral cross which bears the words "light" and "life" in Greek. This is Christ's gift to us, and what we are called to be in the world.

The final leg of the diocesan pilgrimage took place at Saint Stephen's, Dalmuir, where members of the parish youth group led a short prayer service for pupils of Saint Stephen's primary school. After the large-scale hustle and bustle of the city pilgrimage, it felt entirely appropriate that the last word went to the children who will be the next generation of young people, the next followers of Christ.

It was also poignant to finish in Saint Stephen's because of the recent death of Christine McColl, a parishioner and member of the World Youth Day pilgrimage group, who died in January. We prayed for Christine and her family at each point on the Cross's journey through the diocese.

For some of us this journey was the moment when the fruits of the World Youth Day experiences literally came home. It was great to see that so many of those pilgrims from Paris, Rome and Toronto are still involved in their parishes, or just living out their baptismal vocations in the workplace with passion, generosity and humour.

Undoubtedly for some it was a good day off school and has since receded into ancient history. But for most it was an experience rich with reflections and insights into what it means to carry the cross as a young Catholic in today's Glasgow.

The cross is a gift from God—a difficult gift for us to accept, understand and carry. But it is the instrument which puts skin on our beliefs. As Archbishop Conti observed, there is more to the Christian story than nice words. "The Passion of Christ teaches us that following the Way of Jesus is no escapist fantasy, no soft option," he said. "Many warm and sentimental words are attributed to Jesus and His message of love, but surely the most eloquent and real illustration of the meaning of love is Jesus's commitment to you and to me from the Cross. It is a harsh and dreadful love, but one that makes a real difference in every aspect of our lives".

In our pilgrimage with the Cross through Glasgow, our young people took the symbol of our faith and made it real by placing their hands and their skin on it.

If our pilgrimage with the cross through life is to be real, then we need to make flesh the love of God for others.

The Past, the Present, and the Future

Pope John Paul II Evaluates World Youth Days

In his letter of 8 May 1996 to Cardinal Eduardo Francisco Pironio, Pope John Paul II comments on a seminar on World Youth Days that is being held in Czestochowa, Poland. The letter provides good insight into the high value the Pope places on World Youth Days and their importance for the youth of the world:

> It was with great joy that I learnt that the Pontifical Council for the Laity had organized at the Shrine of Jasna Góra, Czestochowa, a Seminar on World Youth Days.
>
> I am very pleased at this initiative and could not let it pass without offering a word of encouragement to the participants, and also expressing my grateful appreciation for all that has been done for the young people of the world.
>
> Firstly, how can we not thank God for the numerous fruits produced by World Youth Days on many different levels? The first meeting held in Saint Peter's Square on Palm Sunday 1986, started a tradition of world and diocesan gatherings in alternate years, underlining, as it were, the twofold dimension, local and universal, of young people's indispensable apostolic commitment.
>
> The Days in fact were born, also in response to an initiative of young people themselves, of a desire to offer them a significant "break" on the on-going pilgrimage of faith, which is indeed nurtured by meetings with young people of other nations and sharing respective experiences.

The principal objective of the Days is to make the person of Jesus the centre of the faith and life of every young person so that he may be their constant point of reference and also the inspiration of every initiative and commitment for the education of the new generations. This is the slogan of every Youth Day, and through this decade, the Days have been like an uninterrupted and pressing call to build life and faith upon the rock, who is Christ.

So young people are called periodically to make a pilgrimage along the roads of the world. In young people the Church sees herself and her mission to mankind: with them she faces the challenges of the future, aware that all humanity needs to be rejuvenated in spirit. This pilgrimage of the young members of the people builds bridges of brotherhood and hope between continents, peoples and cultures. It is a journey which is always in action, like life, like youth.

With the passing years, World Youth Days have proved themselves to be not conventional rites, but providential events, occasions for young people to profess and proclaim faith in Christ with ever greater joy. Coming together, they are able to discuss their most intimate aspirations, experience the Church as communion, make a commitment to the urgent task of new evangelization. And in doing so, they join hands, forming an immense circle of friendship, uniting in faith in the Risen Lord all the different races and nations, cultures and experiences.

World Youth Day is the Church's Day for youth and with youth. This idea is not an alternative to ordinary youth ministry, often carried out with great sacrifice and self-denial. Indeed it intends actually to consolidate this work by offering new encouragement for commitment, objectives which foster ever greater involvement and participation. By aiming to foster greater fervour in apostolate among young people, on no account the Church desires to isolate them from the rest of the community, but rather make them the protagonists of an apostolate which will spread to the other ages and situations of life in the ambit of "new evangelization".

The different moments of which a Youth Day is composed, form a sort of prolonged catechesis, a proclamation of the path of conversion to Christ, starting from the deepest experiences and questions of the daily life of the addressees. The Word of God is the central point, catechetical reflection is the method, prayer is the nutriment, and communication and dialogue, the style.

A Youth Day offers a young person a vivid experience of faith and communion, which will help to face the profound questions of life and to responsibly assume his or her place in society and in the ecclesial community.

During these unforgettable Youth Meetings, I have often been deeply touched by young peoples' joyous, spontaneous love for God and for the Church. They tell of suffering borne for the Gospel, of apparently irremovable obstacles overcome with God's help: they speak of their anguish before a world tormented by despair, cynicism and conflict. Each new Meeting, leaves me with an ever greater desire to praise God for revealing to young ones the secrets of his Kingdom (see *Matthew* 11:25).

The experience of Youth Days is an invitation to all of us, Bishops and pastoral workers, to constant reflection on our ministry among young people and the responsibility which we have to present to them the whole truth about Christ and his Church.

How can we not interpret their massive, willing and enthusiastic participation, as a constant demand to be accompanied on the pilgrimage of faith, on the journey which they undertake in response to God's grace working in their hearts?

They ask us to lead them to Christ, the only One who has words of eternal life (cf. *John* 6:68). Listening to young people and teaching them, requires attention, time and wisdom. Youth ministry is one of the Church's priorities on the threshold of the third millennium.

With their enthusiasm and their exuberant energy, young people ask to be encouraged to become "leading characters in evangelization and participants in the renewal of society" (*Christifideles Laici,* number 46). In this way young people, in whom the Church recognises her own youth as the Bride of Christ (cf. *Ephesians* 5:22–33), are not only evangelized, they also become evangelizers who carry the Gospel to their peers, even to those who do not know the Church and have not yet heard the Good News.

While I exhort all those responsible for youth ministry to make use of World Youth Days, with ever greater generosity and creativity, as events which, inserted in the normal process of education in the faith, may become the privileged manifestation of the whole Church's attention for the young generations and her confidence in them, I hope that the meeting in Czestochowa will help and stimulate the participants' reflection so that they may discover new and more efficacious ways of proposing the faith to young people.

Entrusting the work of the Seminar to the powerful intercession of Our Lady of Jasna Góra, Mother of young people, I gladly impart to you, Your Eminence, your collaborators, the participants and all whom they represent and carry in their hearts, my special Apostolic Blessing.

Preparations and a Glimpse Ahead

Mystery is sometimes a forgotten experience in today's world. Yet it is often through mystery that we become most aware of God's presence and movement in our lives.

The World Youth Days—these gatherings of young people to celebrate their faith, the almost tangible love between the Pope and the young people who adore him, the challenges and commitments to a deeper life of faith, and the incredible sacrifice and dedication of adults in ministry with the young—are certainly mysteries.

Those who experience these World Youth Day celebrations are often at a loss for words to describe their experience. Gottfried Wölfl describes World Youth Day as he experienced it:

> It is now already ten years ago, but I still hear him [the Pope] speaking to the crowd. No, he was not speaking to a bunch of youngsters or a special group! No, he spoke to each one of us personally. He spoke to our hearts!

After the papal Mass at Downsview Park in Toronto, Ontario, Canada, Pope John Paul II announced that the next World Youth Day would be held in Cologne, Germany, in 2005:

> In the great Cathedral in Cologne are honoured the relics of the Magi, the Wise Men from the East who followed the star which led them to Christ. As pilgrims, your spiritual journey to Cologne starts today. Christ awaits you there for the Twentieth World Youth Day! May the Virgin Mary, our Mother on our pilgrimage of faith, be with you on the way. (XVII World Youth Day 2002)

At the writing of this book, preparations are well under way for the 2005 international celebration of World Youth Day. Its theme is "We have come to worship Him"

(*Matthew* 2:2). The cathedral in Cologne is the place where, for centuries, the relics of the three Magi have been venerated, and this is the city where the youth of the world will gather once more. The pilgrimage to Cologne has begun; thousands of young people from around the world are praying, preparing, fund-raising, and planning for their once-in-a-lifetime trip, and have been doing so for a very long time.

The 10 April 2004 issue of the official newsletter for World Youth Day 2005 detailed the hard work of the people of Germany as they prepare to welcome the youth of the world. During Palm Sunday ceremonies in 2004, Kathrin Dennstedt, a Berlin-based member of the Association of German Catholic Youth, addressed some special words to the Pope via live satellite link:

> You have great faith in the young generation, and we are grateful to you. The young people of Germany are looking forward to your visit! Come and see us! Tell us about your journey with Christ! Encourage us once again to bear witness to His truth.

The office in Cologne has been at work for many months as it prepares to welcome the young pilgrims to World Youth Day XX. Training volunteers, providing seminars on intercultural learning, scheduling the Cross as it travels throughout Europe and Germany, planning social outreach experiences and providing a newsletter on World Youth Day have kept them focused and busy looking towards the future of the event itself. Host parishes and families in the "Days in the Diocese" experience preceeding World Youth Day are being contacted and invited to give of their own unique hospitality to the world's young people. And as the months unfold, preparation will increase and excitement will grow as young people and those who accompany them prepare for the pilgrimage to Köln.

Soon, and in years to come, the young people of the world will gather once again with their Pope to share in the Good News of Jesus and to share in the mystery of faith . . . the work of the Holy Spirit . . . their passion for the young Church . . . the joy of youth . . . years of tradition . . . the excitement of something new . . . the hope for the future . . . World Youth Day!

See you in Cologne! See you at the World Youth Days to come!

Contributors

Kathleen A. Carver is an associate director for the National Federation for Catholic Youth Ministry (NFCYM). Her major responsibilities include coordinating all NFCYM publications, the Second Wind program, the National Youth Congress, and the work of NFCYM's certification and accreditation committee. Kathy has been married for seventeen years to Bruce Baumgarten, and they are the proud parents of twelve-year-old Christine Carver Baumgarten.

Robert Collins is a full-time youth minister at Saint John the Evangelist Church in Wellesley, Massachusetts, as well as a part-time student at Saint John's Seminary in Brighton, Massachusetts. Bob is married to Charlene, his best friend in high school, and lives in Wrentham, Massachusetts.

Chris Docherty is the youth development officer for the Archdiocese of Glasgow, Scotland. He has attended World Youth Days in Paris, Rome, and Toronto.

Andrei Gotia is teaching Latin and Greek at the International Theological Institute in Gaming, Austria, and is finishing his doctoral thesis in the classics. He was born in Cluj-Napoca, Romania, and he is a Byzantine Catholic.

Paul Henderson is the executive director of the publishing office for the United States Conference of Catholic Bishops (USCCB). During the past fifteen years at the USCCB, he has worked extensively in youth and young adult ministry and for the Jubilee Year 2000.

Rafael Hernández Urigüen es Capellán Universitario, Doctor en Teología y Profesor de Ética y Teología en ISSA (Instituto Superior de Secretariado y Administración de la Universidad de Navarra), San Sebastián, España.

Melissa Hines is a youth minister at Corpus Christi Catholic Church in Tampa, Florida. She graduated from the Franciscan University of Steubenville (Ohio) with a double major in humanities-Catholic culture and theology. She loves her job with the Corpus Christi teens and enjoys reading, traveling, and visiting with family on her days off.

Nicholas Huck graduated from the University of Richmond (Virginia) and is a part of Alliance for Catholic Education at Notre Dame University. Besides playing basketball, running, and hiking, he enjoys reading, writing letters, and telling jokes.

Colette A. Kennett has been involved in youth ministry for over thirty years in the Diocese of Belleville (Illinois). Colette enjoys creative opportunities, cultural experiences, and cheering on those Saint Louis Cardinals!

Gail Lubahn attended her first World Youth Day in Toronto in 2002. She taught school for over twenty years. Gail and her husband, Steve, proudly parent their daughter, Kelli.

Charles Mwongera is a theology student at Saint Thomas Aquinas Major Seminary in Kenya and intends to become a Catholic priest. Charles is a black Kenyan citizen who loves life.

Anthony Ramuscak is a student at Saint Jean de Brebeuf school in Hamilton, Ontario, Canada. He received his calling to the priesthood at birth.

Gottfried Wölfl is from Austria and has served youth in a variety of settings. After an orientation experience in France, he will spend fourteen months working with young people in Manila, Philippines, through the Catholic organization Points Cœur.

Acknowledgments

The scriptural quotations labeled NRSV contained herein are from the New Revised Standard Version of the Bible, Catholic Edition. Copyright © 1993 and 1989 by the Division of Christian Education of the National Council of the Churches of Christ in the United States of America. All rights reserved.

The quotations from the Second Vatican Council on pages 10–11 and 18 are from "Message of the II Vatican Council to Youth" at *www.vatican.va/gmg/documents/gmg-2002_ii-vat-council_message-youth_19651207_en.html*, accessed 26 May 2004.

The material in "Truth," "Moral Formation and Ethics," "The Sacraments," "Vocations," "Freedom," "Love," and "The Challenge" on pages 15–18 is paraphrased from the following messages to youth from Pope John Paul II: XII World Youth Day (WYD) 1997; International Youth Year, 1985; XII WYD 1997; VIII WYD 1993; VI WYD 1991; VIII WYD 1993; IX and X WYD 1994 and 1995, respectively. The text of these messages can be found at *www.vatican.va*.

The excerpt on page 26 is from "Words of John Paul II to Young People" at *www.vatican.va/holy_father/john_paul_ii/speeches/1984/april/documents/hf_jp-ii_spe_19840422_cross-youth_en.html*, accessed 26 May 2004.

The quotations on pages 27 and 29–33 are from "Apostolic Letter *Dilecti Amici* of Pope John Paul II to the Youth of the World on the Occasion of International Youth Year" at *www.vatican.va/holy_father/john_paul_ii/apost_leters/documents/hf_jp-ii_apl_31031985_dilecti-amici_en.html*, accessed 26 May 2004.

The invitations to youth from Pope John Paul II on pages 27–28 are from "World Youth Day," by The Holy See Press Office, at *www.vatican.va/news_services/press/ documentazione/documents/giornate-mondiali/giornata-mondiale-gioventu_elenco_en.html*, accessed 26 May 2004.

The excerpt on page 28 is from *Crossing the Threshold of Hope,* by His Holiness John Paul II (NY: Alfred Knopf, 1994), pages 124–125 and 125. Copyright © 1994 by Arnold Mondadori Editore.

The excerpt on pages 38–42 is from "Message to All Young People on the Occasion of the World Day of Youth II, Palm Sunday 1987 *(Messaggio Di Giovanni Paolo II Per La IV Giornata Mondiale Della Gioventu')* at *www. vatican.va/holy_father/john_paul_ii/messages/youth/ documents/hf_jp-ii_mes_30111986_ii-world-youth-day_it.html*, accessed 27 May 2004.

The words of Pope John Paul II on pages 39 and 59–60 include quotations from *Redemptor Hominis,* numbers 10 and 12, at *www.vatican.va/holy_father/john_paul_ii/ encyclicals/documents/hf_jp-ii_enc_04031979 _redemptor-hominis_en.html*, accessed 8 June 2004.

The excerpt on pages 48–53 is from "Message to the Youth of the World on the Occasion of the Fourth World Youth Day, 1989" *(Messaggio Di Giovanni Paolo II Per La IV Giornata Mondiale Della Gioventu')* at *www.vatican.va/ holy_father/john_paul_ii/messages/youth/documents/hf_jp-ii_mes_27111988_iv-world-youth-day_it.html*, accessed 27 May 2004.

The excerpt on pages 57–63 is from "Message of the Holy Father Pope John Paul II for the VI World Youth Day, 1991" at *www.vatican.va/holy_father/john_paul_ii/ messages/youth/documents/hf_jp-ii_mes_15081990_vi-world-youth-day_en.html*, accessed 26 May 2004.

The words of Pope John Paul II on page 58 include a quotation from *Gaudium et Spes,* number 26, at *www. vatican.va/archive/hist_councils/ii_vatican_council/ documents/vat-ii_cons_19651207_gaudium-et-spes_en.html*, accessed 8 June 2004.

The excerpt on pages 67–72 is from "Message of the Holy Father Pope John Paul II for the VIII World Youth Day, 1993" at *www.vatican.va/holy_father/john_paul_ii/ messages/youth/documents/hf_jp-ii_mes_15081992_viii-world-youth-day_en.html,* accessed 26 May 2004.

The excerpt on pages 77–83 is from "Message of the Holy Father Pope John Paul II for the IX and X World Youth Day" at *www.vatican.va/holy_father/john_paul_ii/ messages/youth/documents/hf_jp-ii_mes_21111993_ix-and-x-world-youth-day_en.html,* accessed 26 May 2004.

The excerpt on pages 87–94 is from "Message of the Holy Father Pope John Paul II to the Youth of the World on the Occasion of the XII World Youth Day, 1997" at *www.vatican.va/holy_father/john_paul_ii/messages/youth/ documents/hf_jp-ii_mes_15081996_xii-world-youth-day_en. html,* accessed 26 May 2004.

The words of Pope John Paul II on page 90 include a quotation from *Lumen Gentium,* number 15, at *www. vatican.va/archive/hist_councils/ii_vatican_council/ documents/vat-ii_const_19641121_lumen-gentium_en.html,* accessed 7 June 2004.

The words of Pope John Paul II on page 92 include a quotation from SaInt Ambrose, *"Epistle* 49: To Sabinus," number 3, at *www.tertullian.org/fathers/ambrose_letters_ 05_letters41_50.htm#Letter49,* accessed 17 August 2004.

The words of Pope John Paul II on pages 93 and 130 include quotations from *Christifideles Laici,* numbers 34 and 46, at *www.vatican.va/holy_father/john_paul_ii/apost_ exhortations/documents/hf_jp-ii_exh_30121988_christifideles-laici_en.html,* accessed 7 June 2004.

The excerpt on pages 98–104 is from "Message of the Holy Father to the Youth of the World on the Occasion of the 15th World Youth Day" at *www.vatican.va/holy_father/ john_paul_ii/messages/youth/documents/hf_jp-ii_mes_ 29061999_xv-world-youth-day_en.html,* accessed 7 June 2004.

The words of Pope John Paul II on page 103 include a quotation from *Incarntionis Mysterium,* number 6, at

*www.vatican.va/jubilee_2000/docs/documents/hf_jp-ii_doc_
30111998_bolla-jubilee_en.html,* accessed 7 June 2004.

The words of Pope John Paul II on page 100 include a quotation from *Evangelium Vitae,* number 50, at *www. vatican.va/edocs/ENG0141/INDEX.HTM,* accessed 7 June 2004.

The excerpt on pages 109–114 is from "Message of the Holy Father to the Youth of the World on the Occasion of the XVII World Youth Day (Toronto 18–28 July 2002)" at *www.vatican.va/holy_father/john_paul_ii/ messages/youth/documents/hf_jp-ii_mes_20010731_xvii-world-youth-day_en.html,* accessed 2 June 2004.

The words of Pope John Paul II on page 112 include a quotation from *Novo Millennio Ineunte,* number 54, at *www.vatican.va/holy_father/john_paul_ii/apost_letters/ documents/hf_jp-ii_apl_20010106_novo-millennio-ineunte_ en.html,* accessed 2 June 2004.

The quotation from Pope John Paul II on page 120 is from the "Angelus" of the XV III World Youth Day, 2003, at *www.vatican.va/holy_father/john_paul_ii/angelus /2003/documents/hf_jp-ii_ang_20030413_en.html,* accessed 8 June 2004.

The excerpt on pages 127–130 is from "Letter of John Paul II to Cardinal Eduardo Francisco Pironio on the Occasion of the Seminar on World Youth Days Organized in Czestochowa" at *www.vatican.va/holy_father/ john_paul_ii/letters/1996/documents/hf_jp-ii_let_19960508_ czestochowa-gmg_en.html,* accessed 26 May 2004.

The announcement by Pope John Paul II in Toronto at XVII WYD 2002 on page 131 is from "20th World Youth Day (Cologne 2005)," by the Pontifical Council for the Laity, at *www.vatican.va/roman_curia/pontifical_councils/ laity/Colonia2005/rc_pc_laity_doc_20030805_homepage-gmg_en.html,* accessed 26 May 2004.

The quotation and the report on the progress of the WYD 2005 on page 132 are from the newsletter of the XX World Youth Day, 10 April 2004, at *wjt2005-newsletter @intersolute.de,* accessed 7 June 2004.

To view copyright terms and conditions for Internet materials cited here, log on to the home pages for the referenced Web sites.

During this book's preparation, all citations, facts, figures, names, addresses, telephone numbers, Internet URLs, and other pieces of information cited within were verified for accuracy. The authors and Saint Mary's Press staff have made every attempt to reference current and valid sources, but we cannot guarantee the content of any source, and we are not responsible for any changes that may have occurred since our verification. If you find an error in, or have a question or concern about, any of the information or sources listed within, please contact Saint Mary's Press.

Photo Credits